I0483395

Paths & Passages

Navigating the Blue Ridge

Paths & Passages

Navigating the Blue Ridge

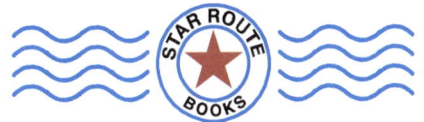

STAR ROUTE BOOKS
SPARTA ★ NORTH CAROLINA

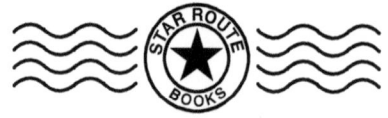

an imprint of Imaging Specialists, Inc.

Copyright © 2012 — Imaging Specialists, Inc.
Sparta, North Carolina

All rights reserved. No part of this book may be reproduced in any form or by electronic or mechanical means, including information page and retrieval systems, without permission in writing from the publisher.

Paths & Passages

NAVIGATING THE BLUE RIDGE

ISBN 978-0-9882647-0-0

First printing, August 2012

WWW.STARROUTEBOOKS.COM

Contents

Number	Name	Page	
1	North Fork	1	
2	Garvey Bridge	2	
3	Garvey Bridge	4	
4	New River	5	(photo pg. 6)
5	Shiloh Rainbow	8	
6	Blue On Blue	9	(photo pg. 10)
7	Morning Fog	12	
8	Green On Green	13	(photo pg. 14)
9	Sunrise Mist	16	
10	Parkway Meadow	18	
11	The Sky Below	20	
12	Unknown Creek at Brush Creek Hall	22	
13	Beaver Dam	24	
14	Duck Pond at Hare Mill	25	(photo pg. 26)
15	The Shire	28	
16	Turning Trees	30	
17	Untitled Tree 3	31	(photo pg. 32)
18	Untitled Tree 4	31	(photo pg. 33)
19	Trespassing	34	
20	Road at Air Bellows	36	
21	Parkway View	36	(photo pg. 38)
22	Waterfall Road	40	
23	Carolyn's Drive	42	
24	Lonesome Pine	44	
25	Crystal Creek	46	
26	Walkway On Water	48	
27	Afternoon Squall	50	
28	The Road Home	52	
29	The Treasure Tree	54	
30	Mr. Green's Farm	55	(photo pg. 56)
31	Moon Shadows	58	

Preface

I always say that you can point a camera in any direction here, in the mountains, and get a good photograph. The Blue Ridge is a beautiful place- unlike any other and some serious artists come here to live and work.

I consider myself an artist- but I'm not all that serious about it. My profession in the graphic arts is serious. I've worked for years in a technical world of cameras, lenses and precision printing processes. There's almost no allowance for fun in pre-press. Clients are darned serious about their reproductions, their registration and their resolution.

If you're a serious artist, if you're a gadget guy who talks only lenses, camera bodies and model numbers, (gadget guys love model numbers), if you're a purist who thinks Photoshop ruined photography-- I apologize in advance. This collection probably won't measure up. Throw the book down and briskly walk away.

These are just some nice scenes, shot for fun, without great meanings or sub-texts.

And these are family efforts. I don't think I've taken many photos in the past thirty years without my wife, Sharon, or at least one of the kids, Claire or Jeremy, along.

I hope you enjoy these images. Not technically perfect, maybe, but perfect enough. Like the places they were shot.

Seriously yours,
Jeff Halsey

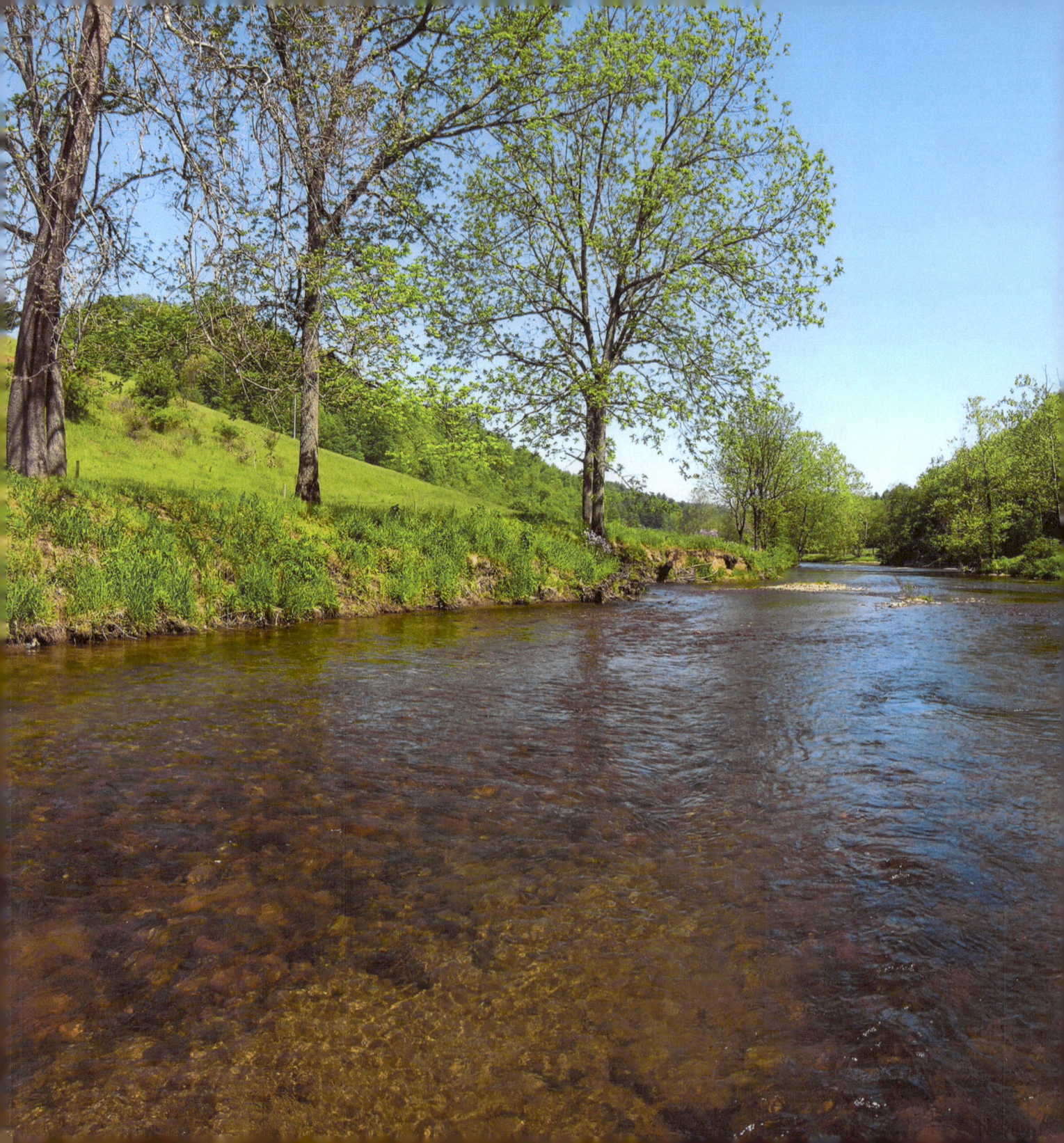

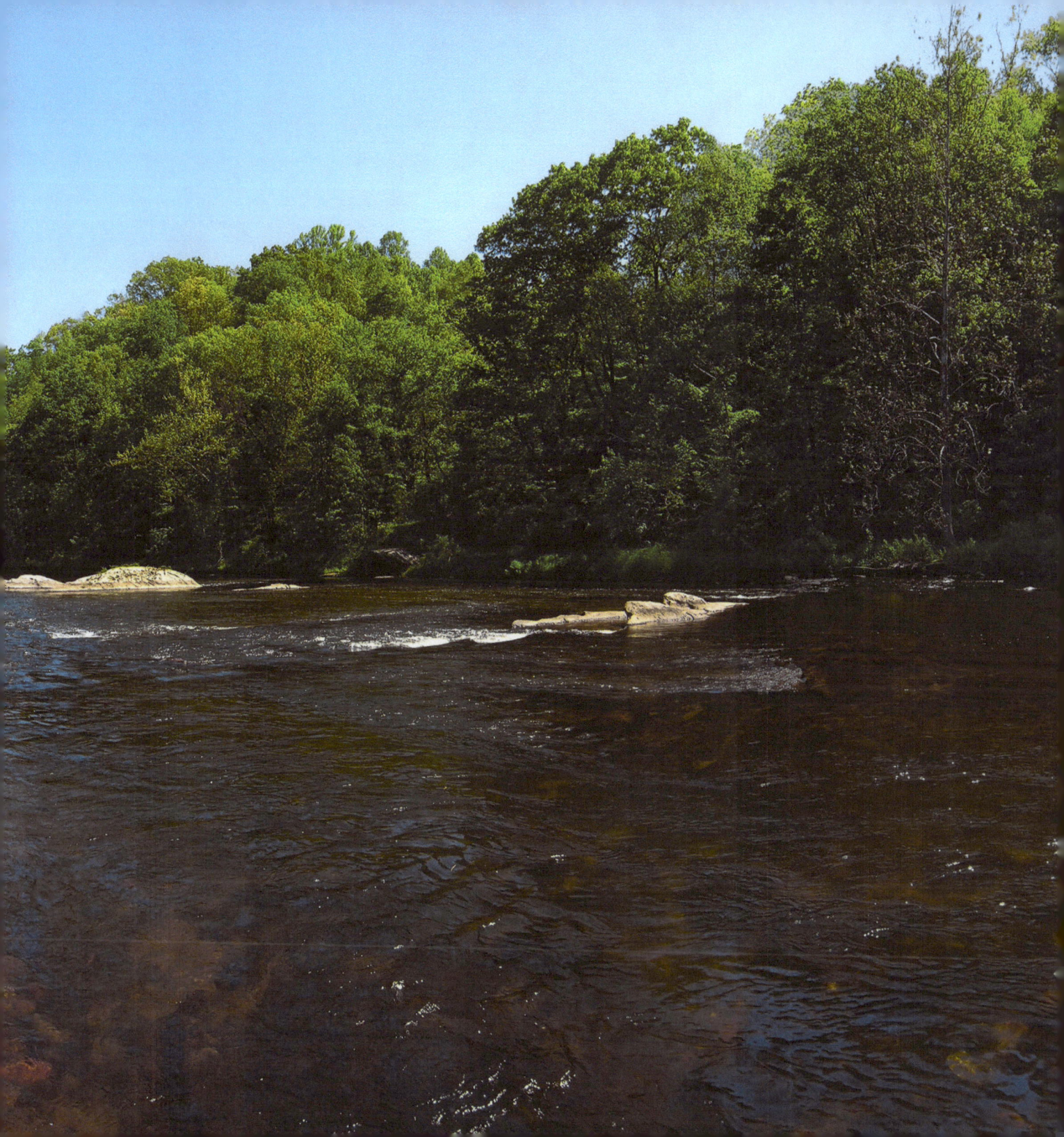

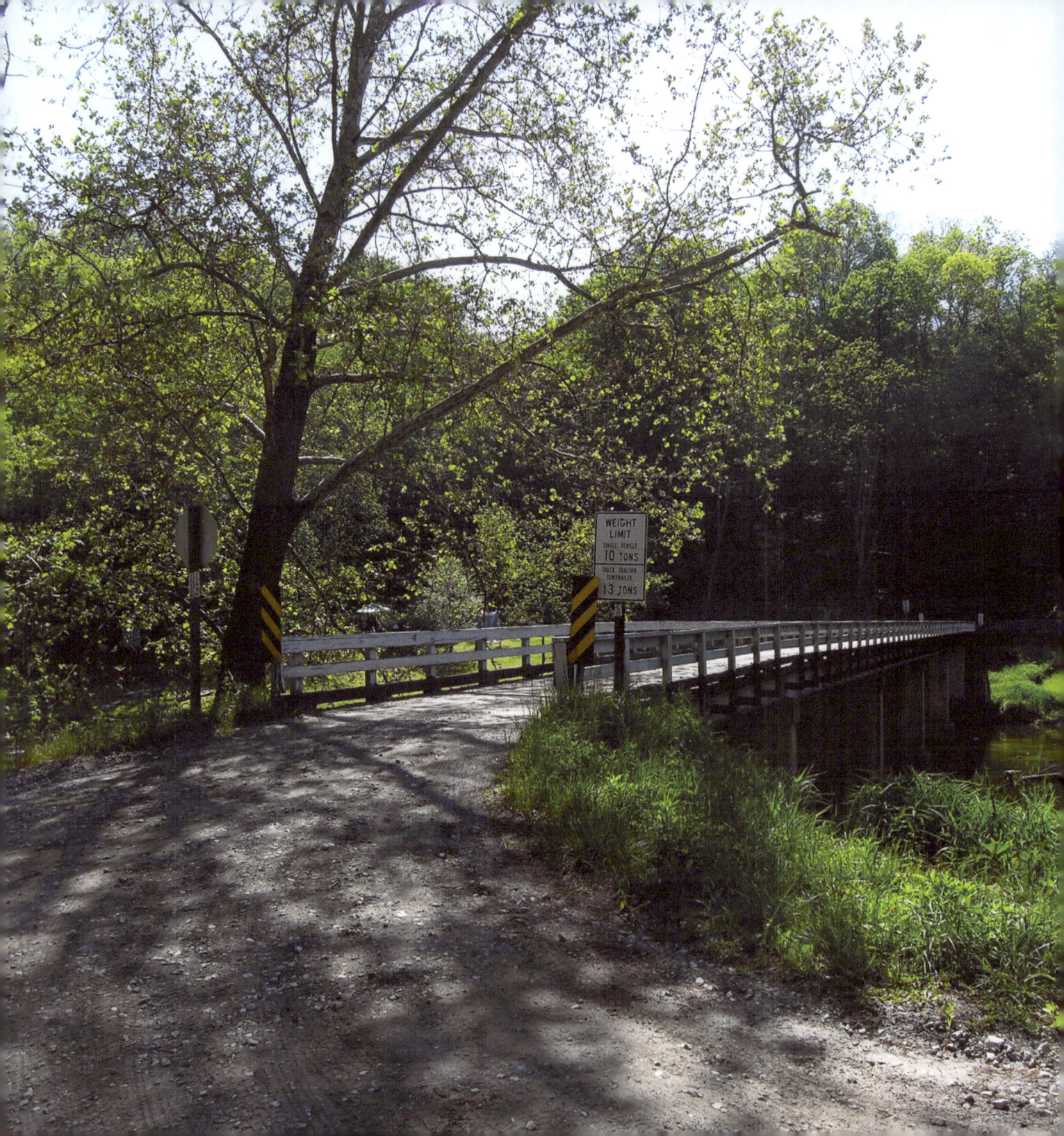

1. **North Fork** of New River. Just above the forks. Sleepy spring afternoon with nothing moving but the River and breezy trees. *(Preceding pages)*

2. **Garvey Bridge** on the north fork of the New River.

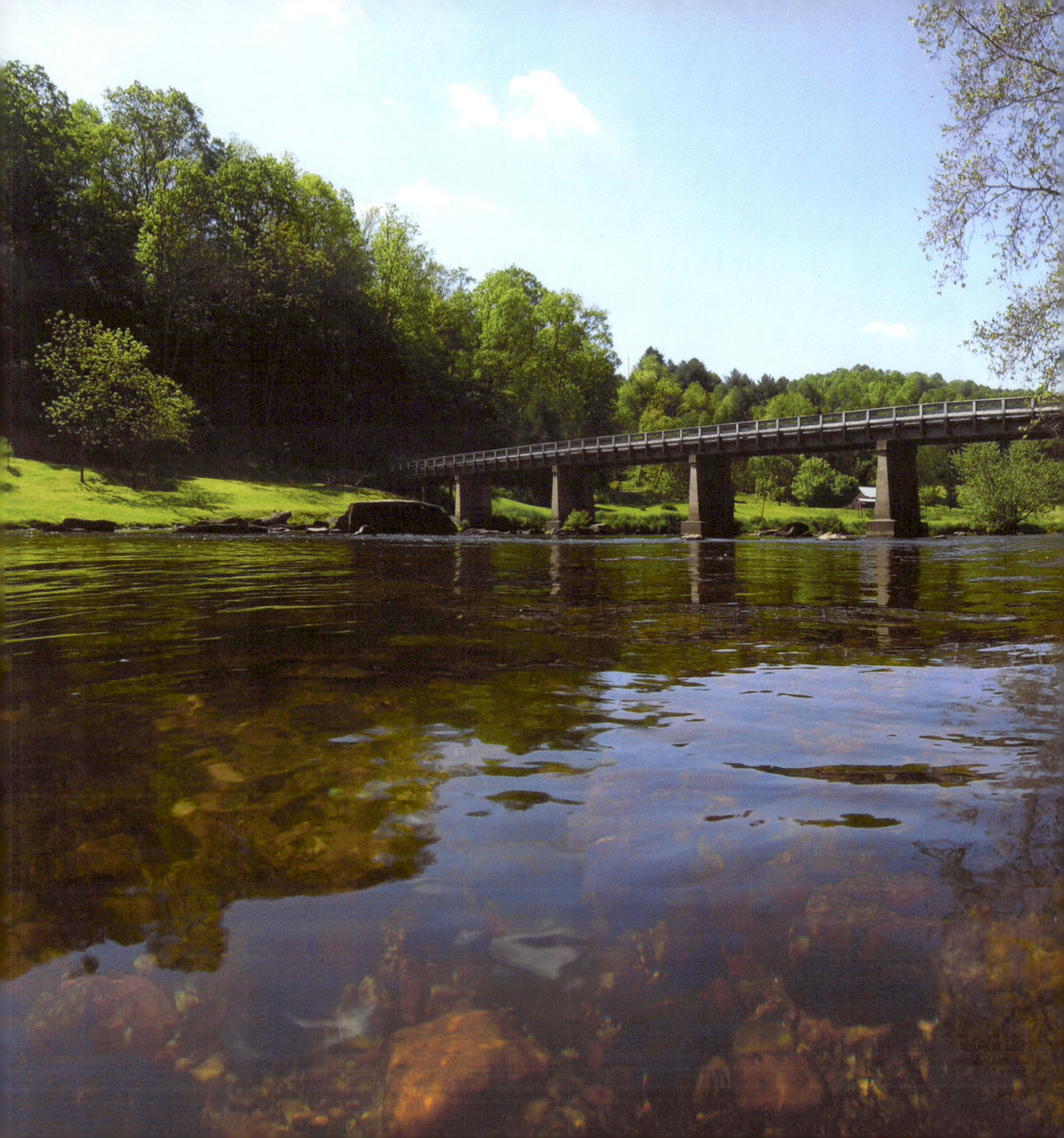

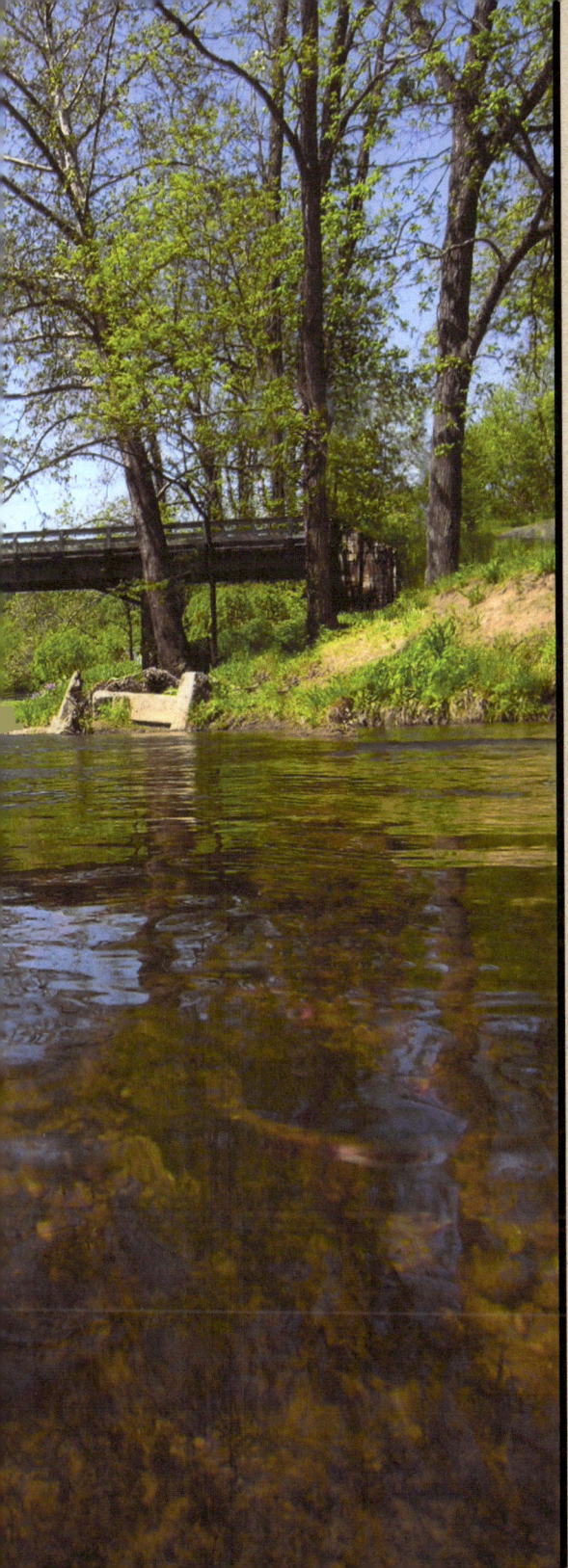

3. **Garvey Bridge** from the river.
I waded out on the slippery rocks with my Nikon, barefoot with no backup plan.

4. **New River.**
Our family lived in this part of the river valley, since the American Revolution. The homeplace is still standing just out of view, beyond the foremost tree on the right bank. *(Following pages)*

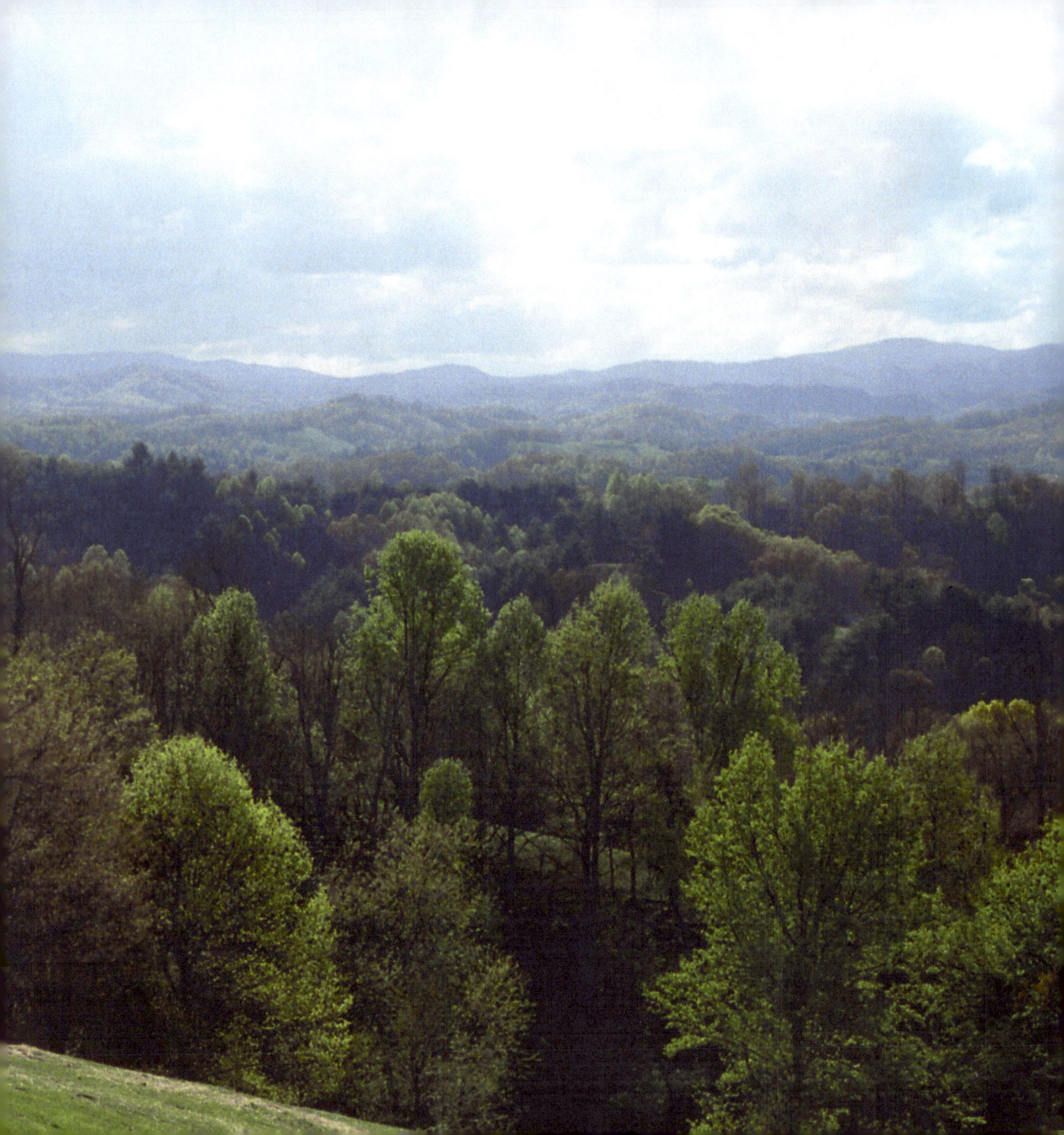

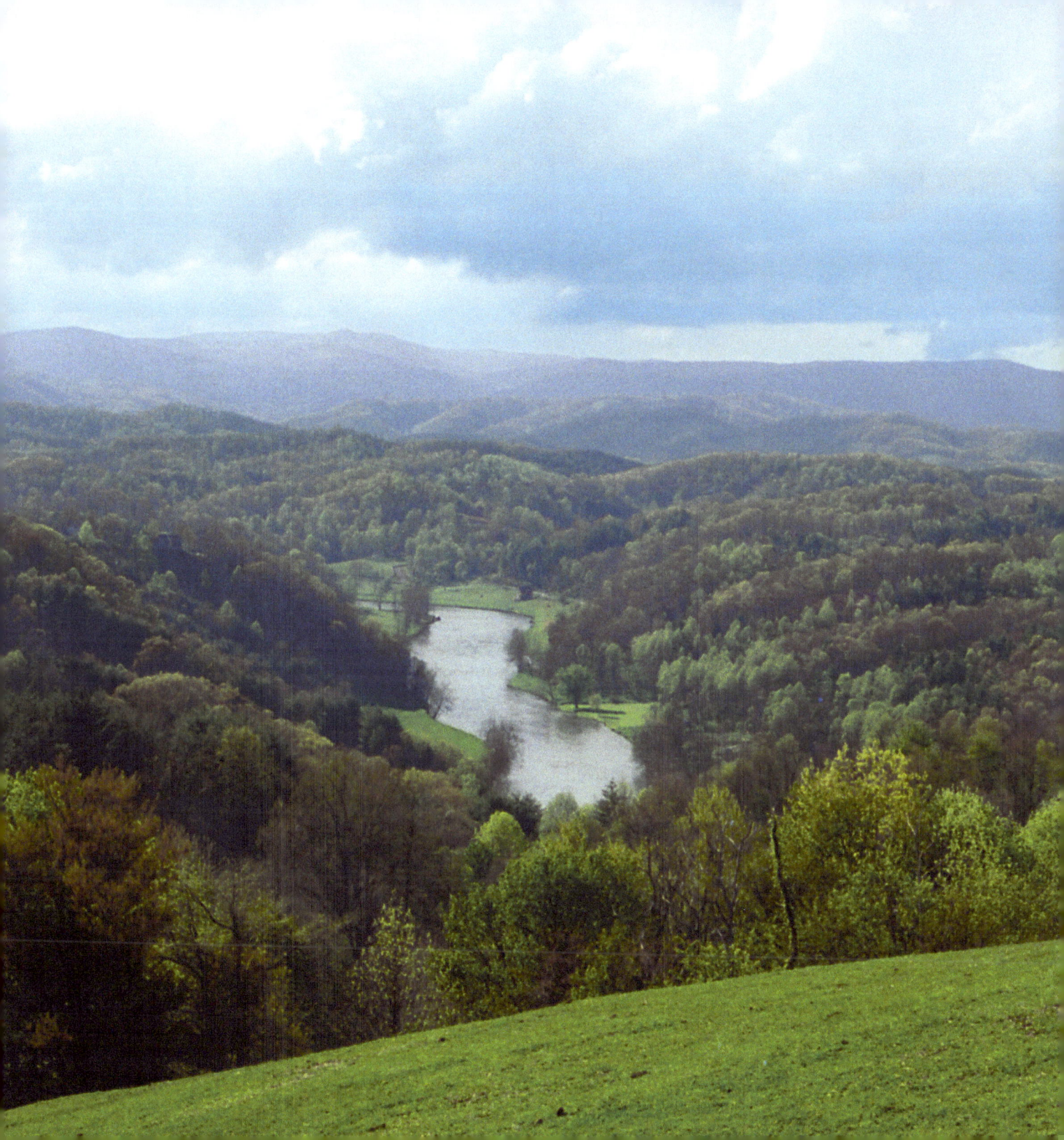

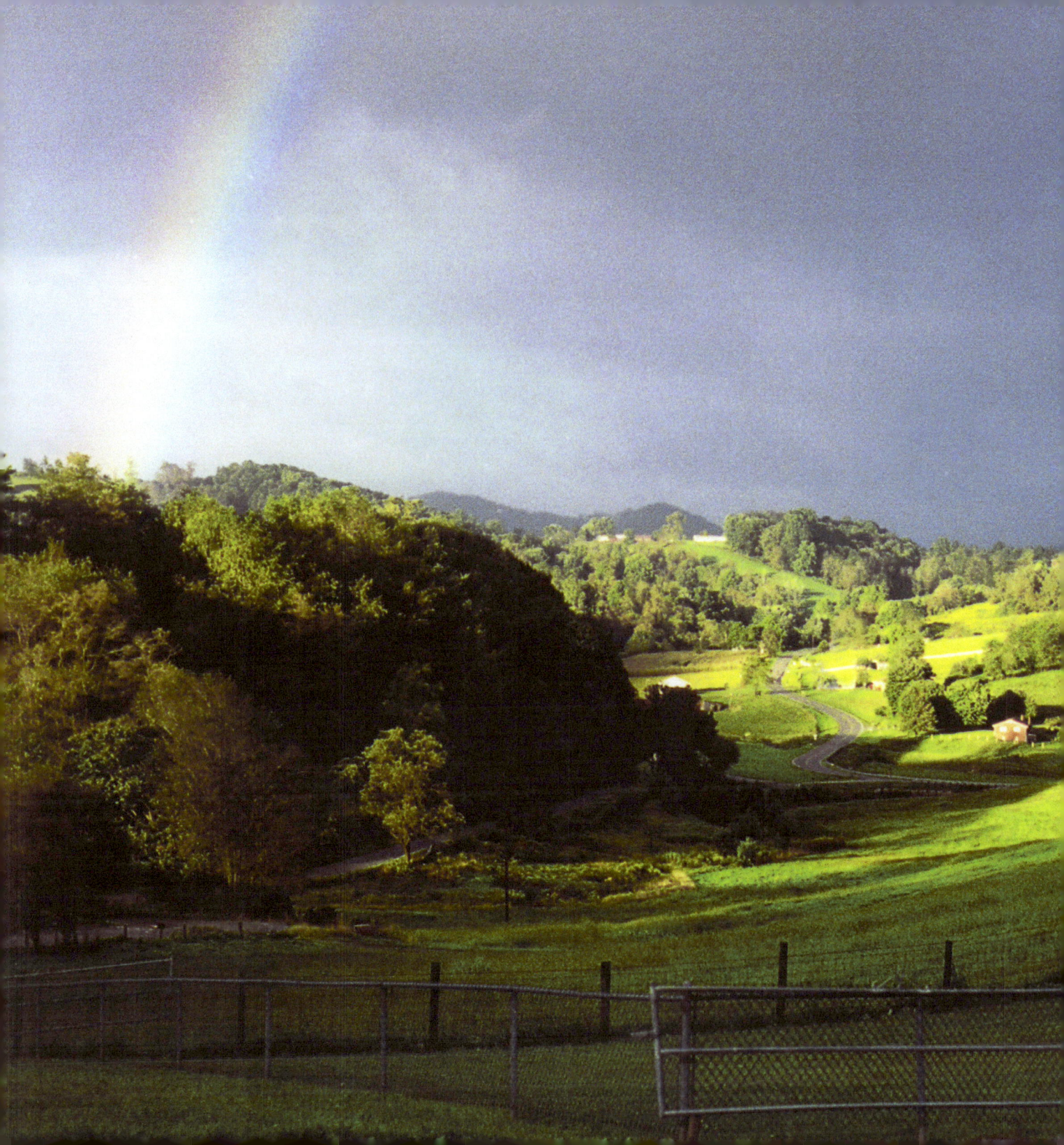

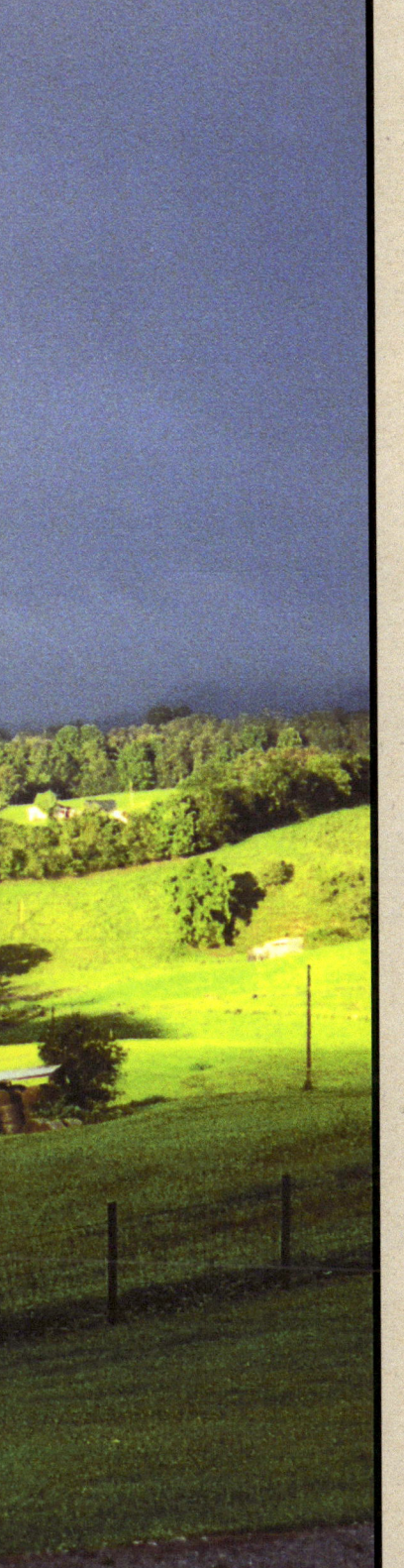

5. **Shiloh Rainbow**.
Highway 221 in front of Shiloh
United Methodist Church. An early
morning storm- with a rainbow
visible at left.

6. **Blue On Blue**.
View from the Parkway, around
milepost 243. Typical morning haze
that gave the mountains their name.
(Following pages)

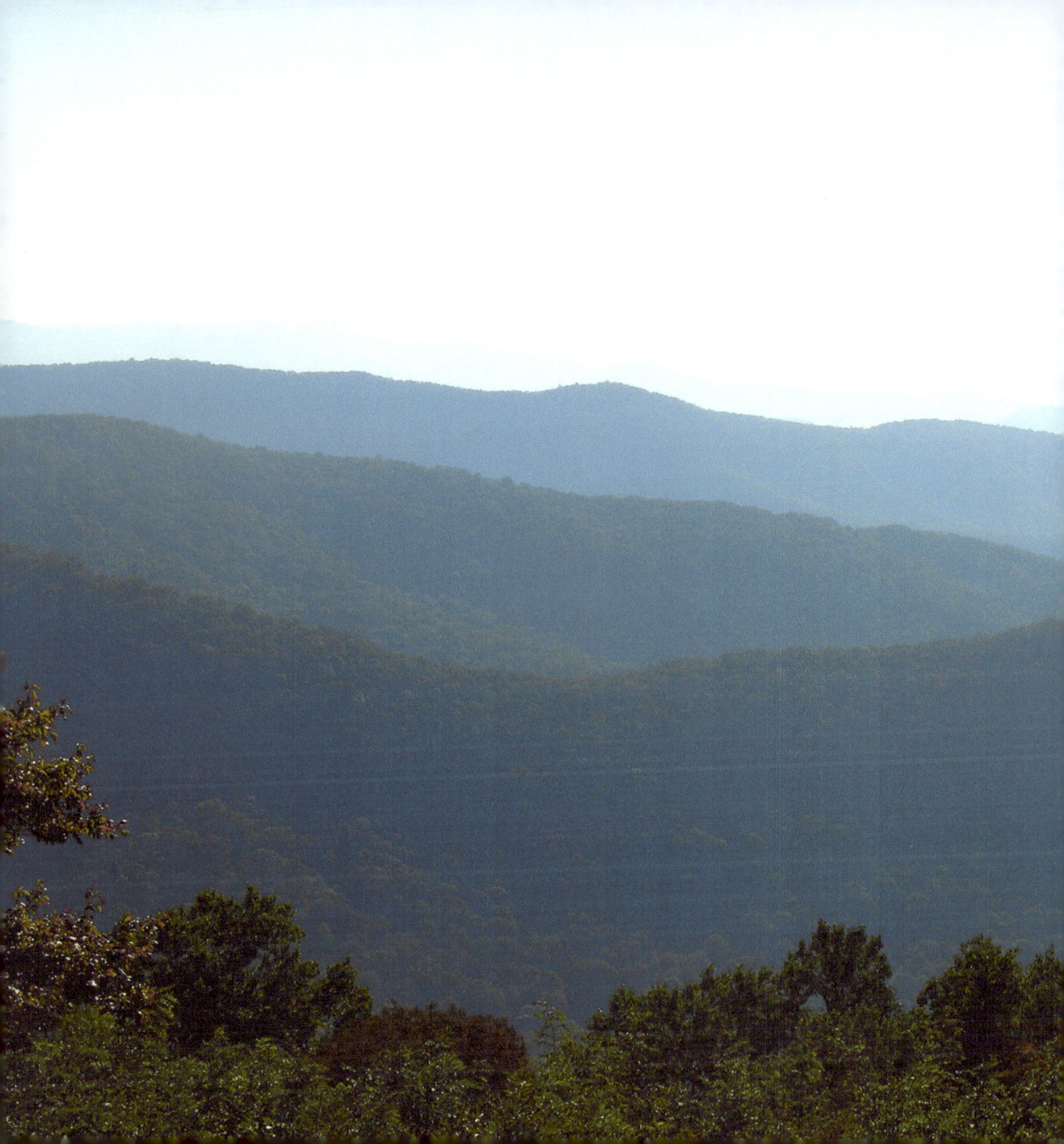

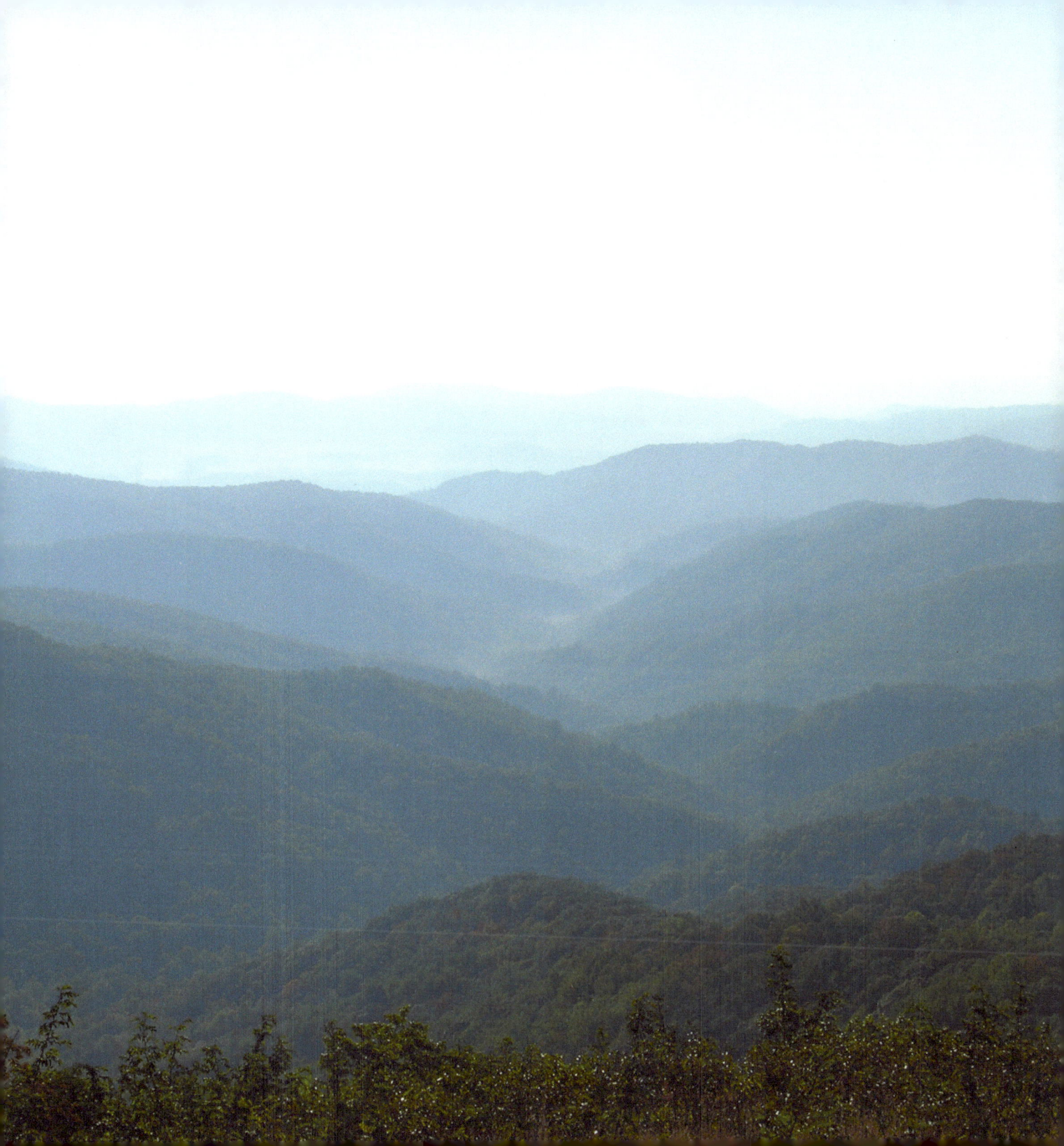

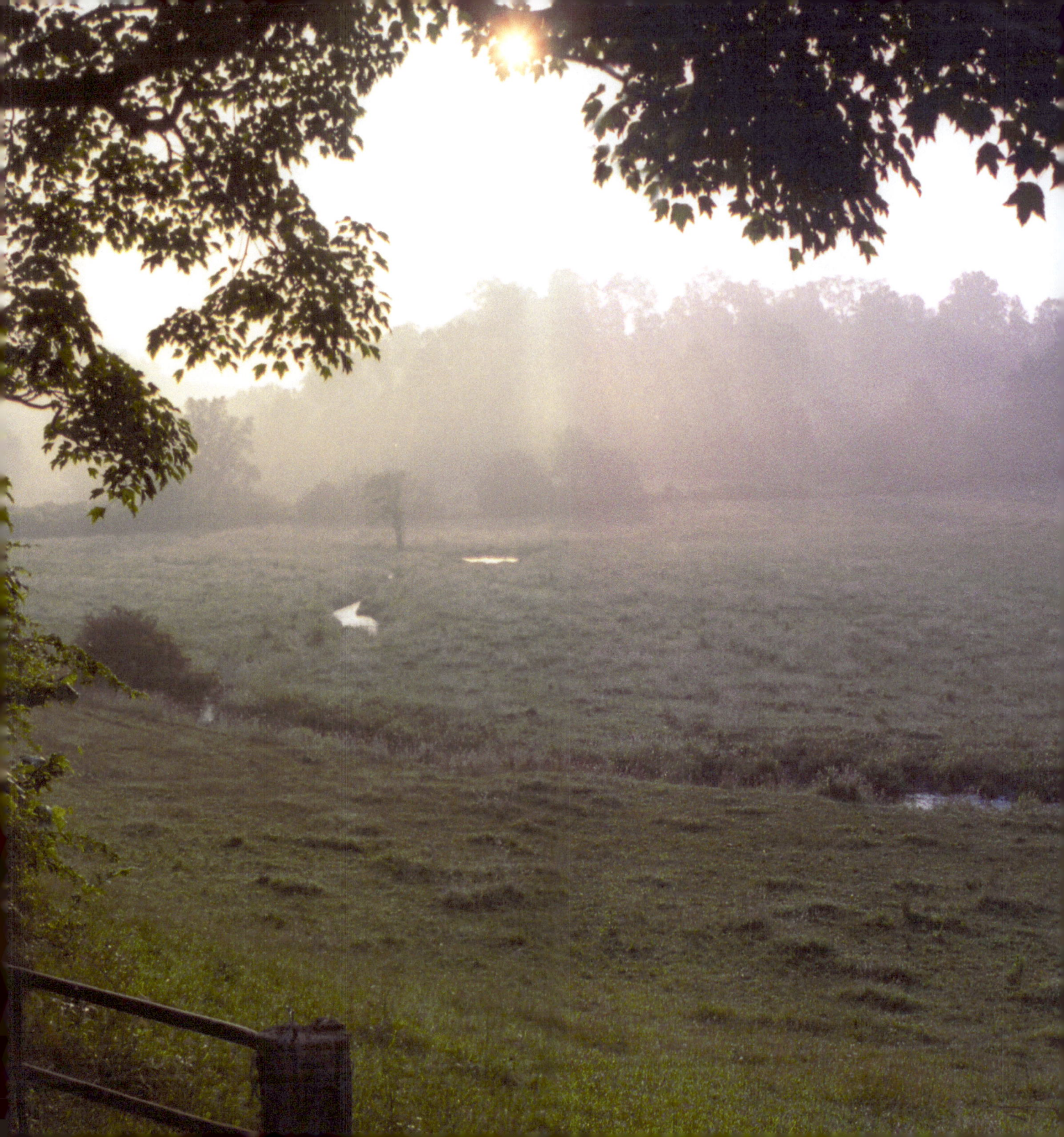

7. **Morning Fog** on Prathers Creek. The bushes along the creek have been cleared away, except for the ones visible at left. Those supported Grandmother's muscadine vines.

8. **Green On Green.**
Along the Fodder Stack Trail at the Bluffs in Doughton Park. The trail is all downhill at the beginning (and uphill coming back, of course) but worth the walk. *(Following pages)*

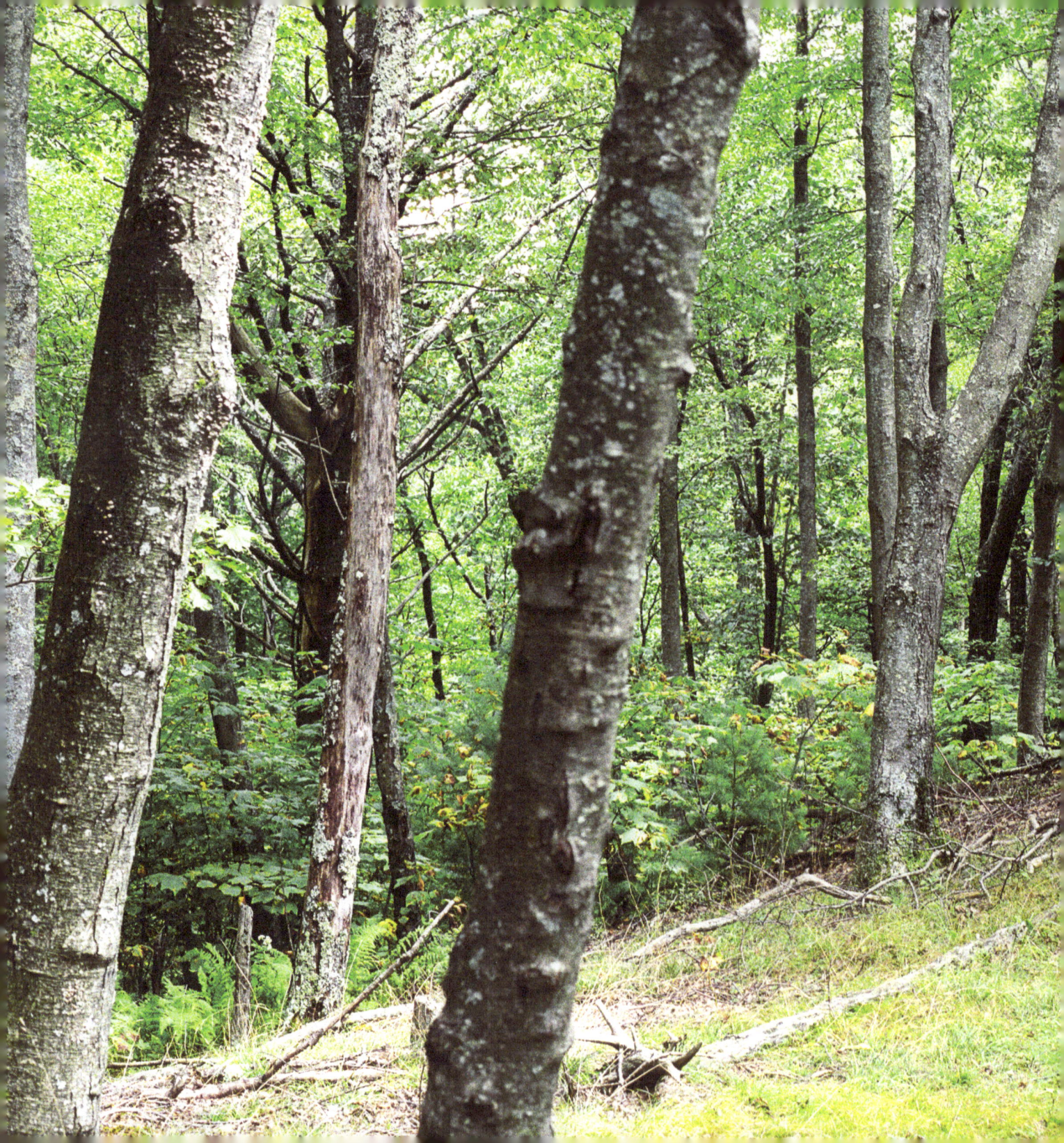

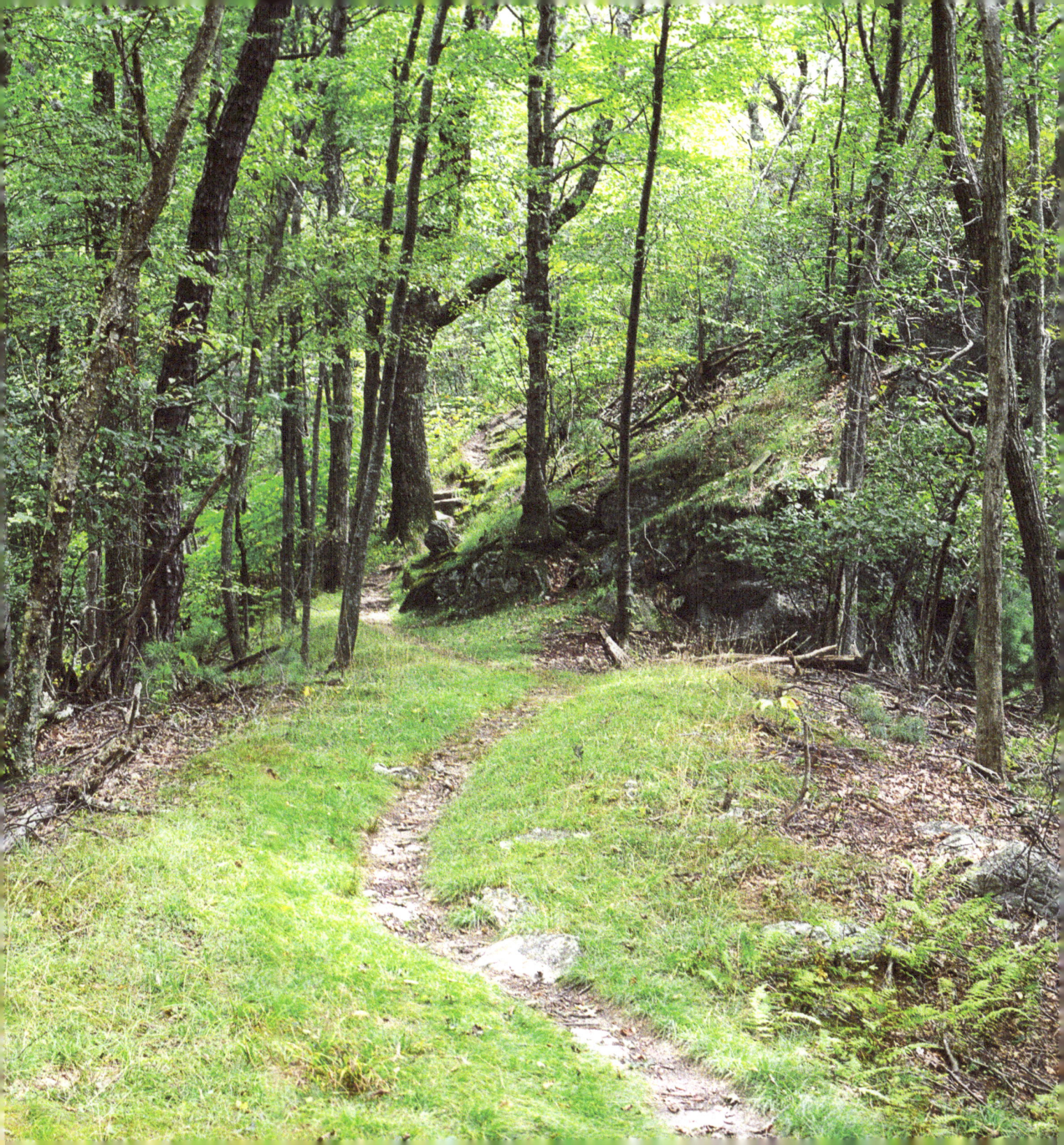

9. **Sunrise Mist.**
   Early morning fog on US 221
   below Twin Oaks.

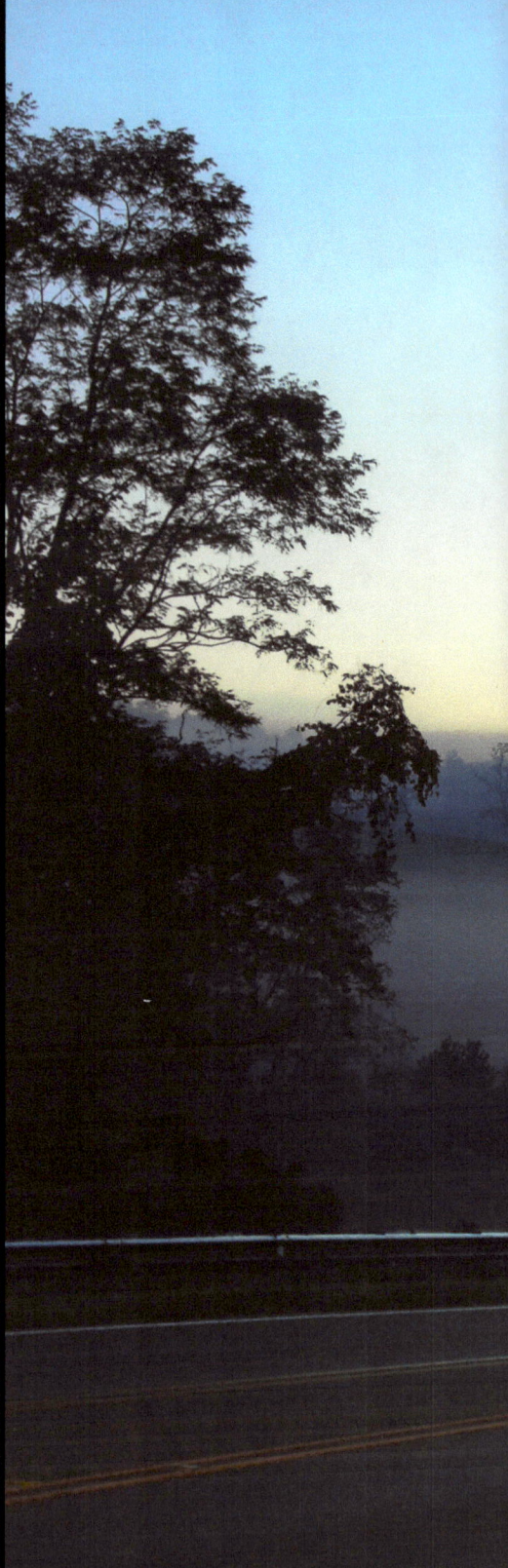

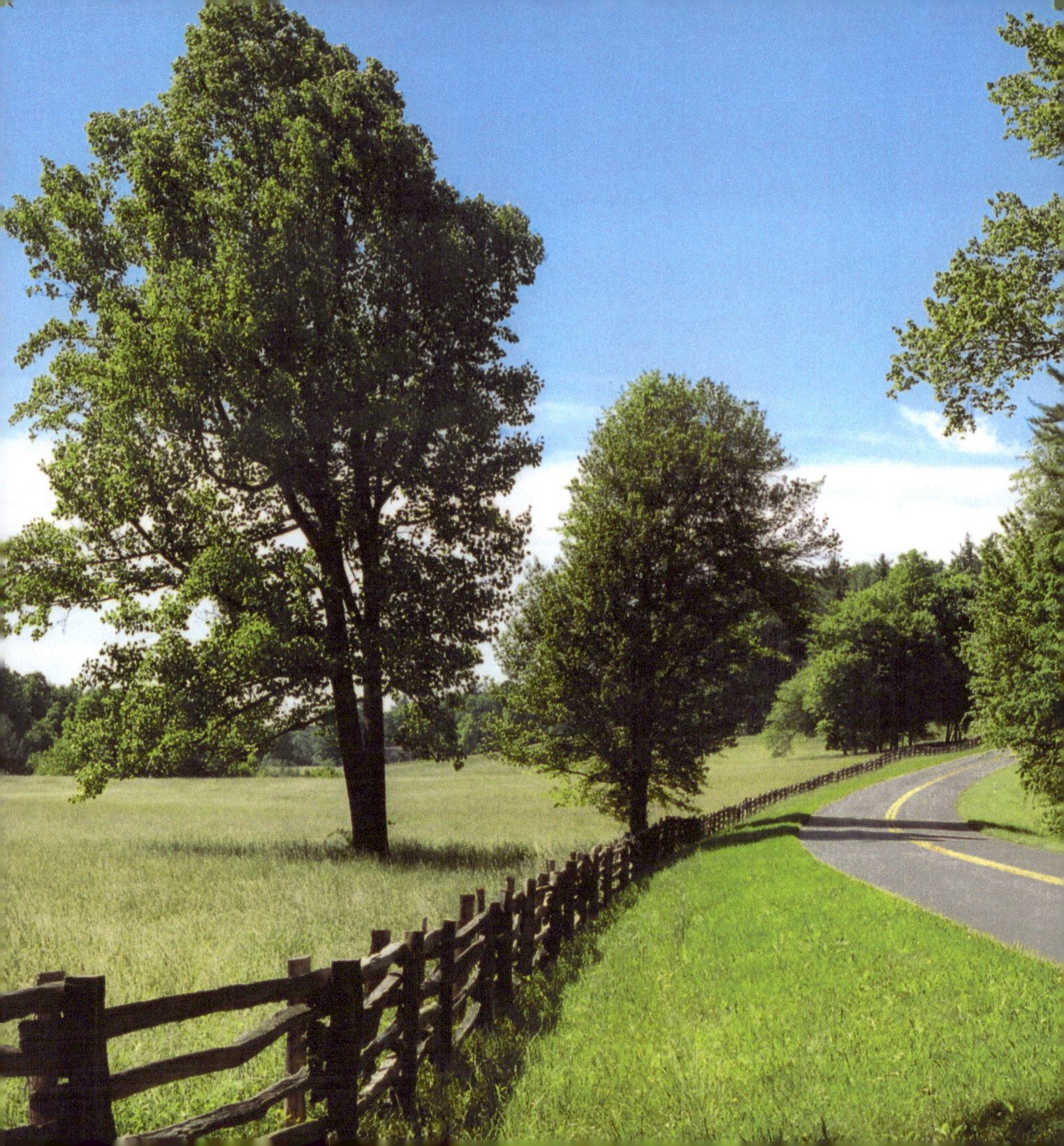

10. **Parkway Meadow**.
High country hay field near the Northwest Trading Post. At milepost 258 in Ashe County.

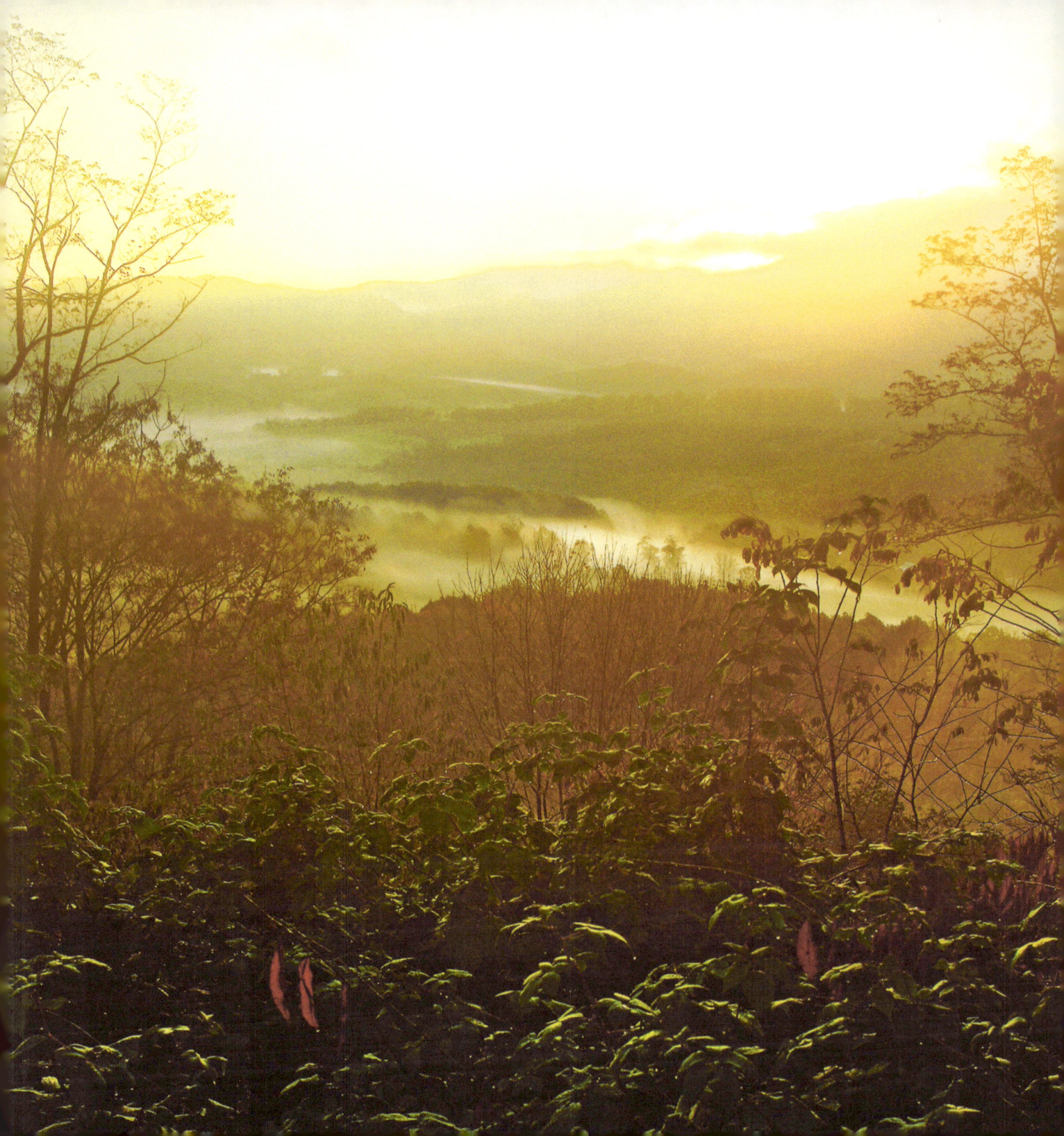

11. The Sky Below.
Shooting straight into the sun is not generally a
great idea but it's what gave us this etherial view.
The horizon is literally lost in the clouds.

12. **Unknown Creek at Brush Creek Hall**.
When asked the name of this creek, Claire said, "Just put down, 'Unknown' - but we shot it beside Brush Creek Hall." If anyone knows the name, please contact Claire.

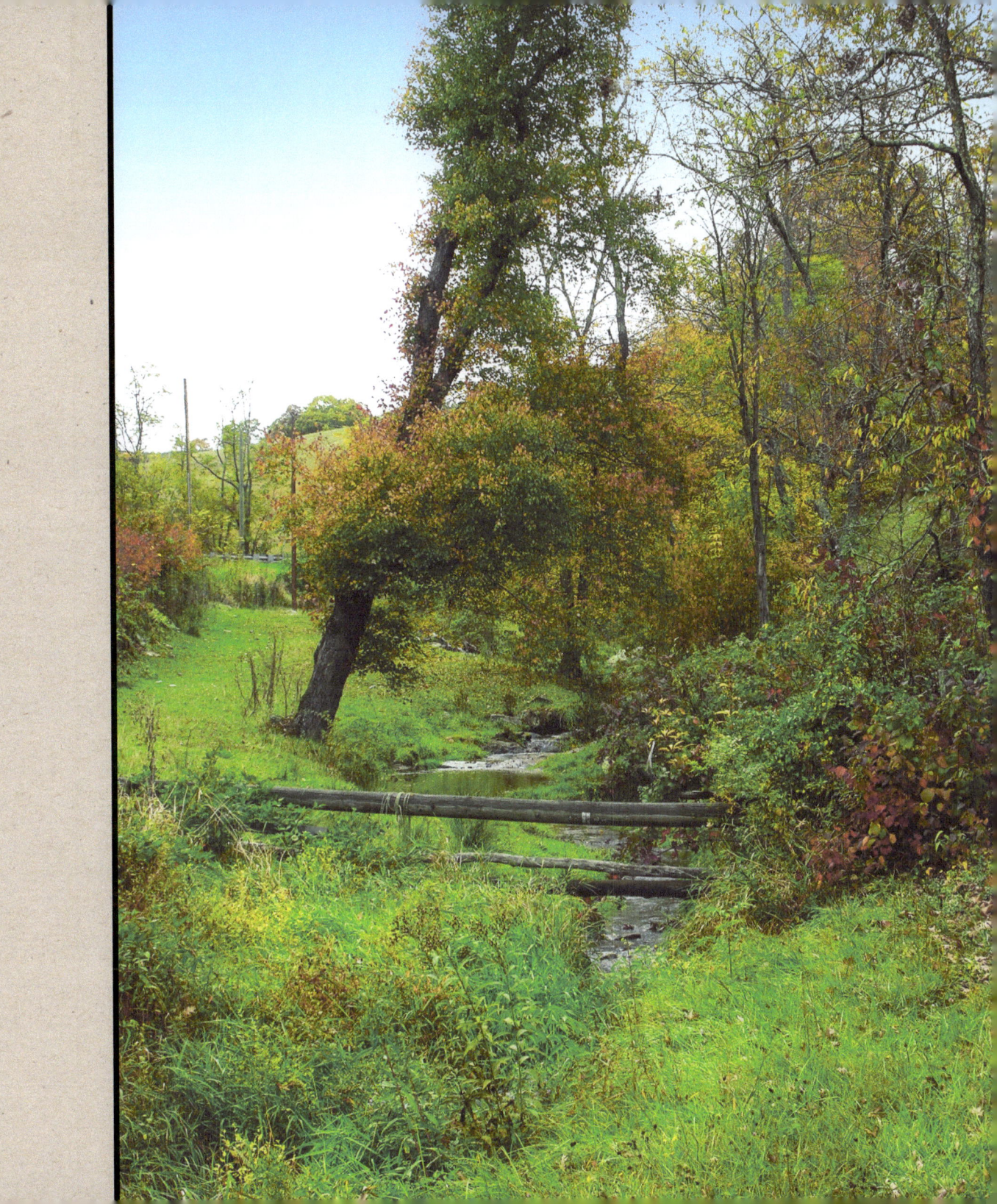

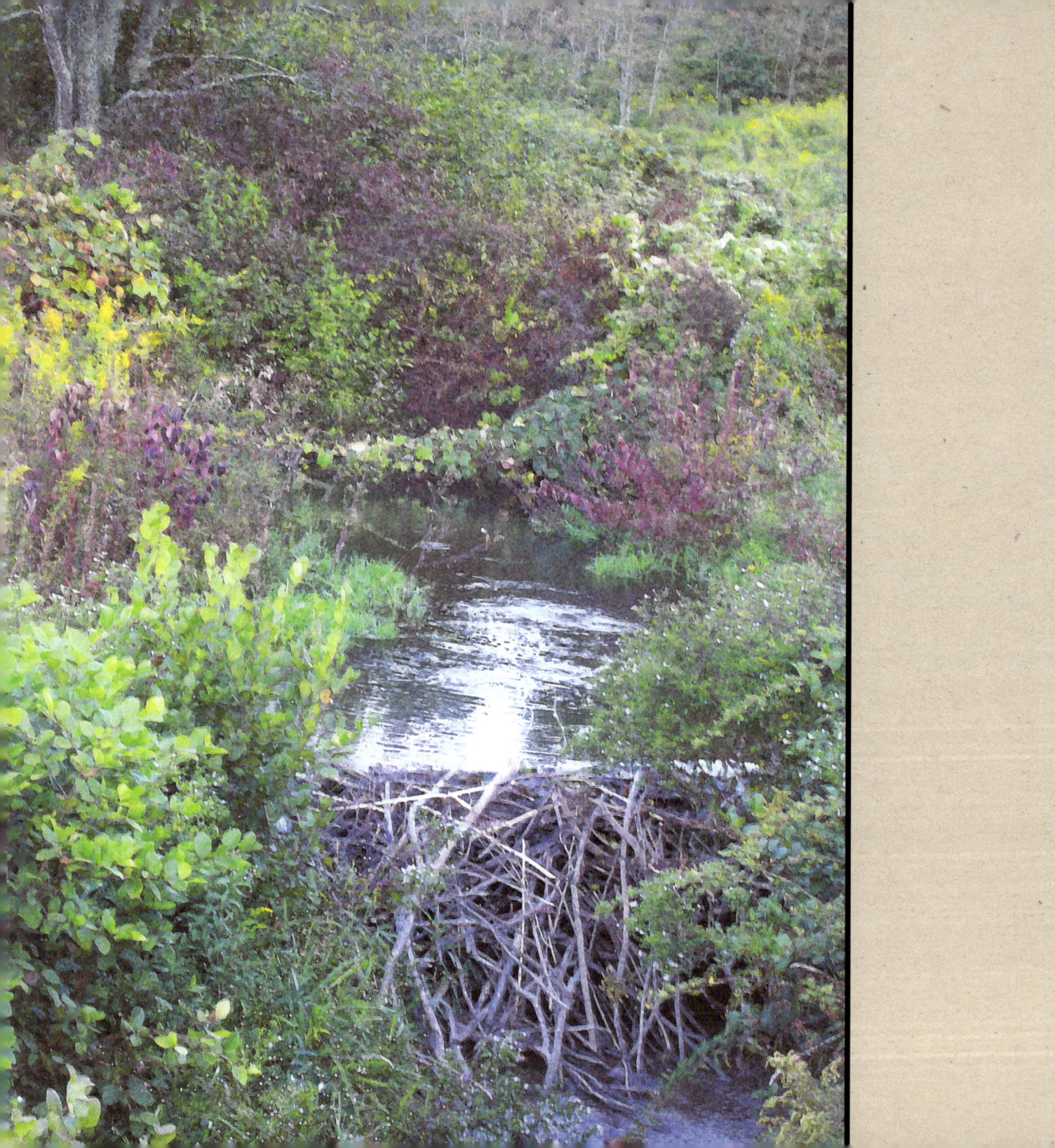

13. **Beaver Dam** on Prathers Creek. Evening photo showing the home of a beaver with a real sense of style.

14. **Duck Pond at Hare Mill**.
Once a mill pond, the Park Service kept it in place and when we found it, I guess it belonged to these two ducks. *(Following pages)*

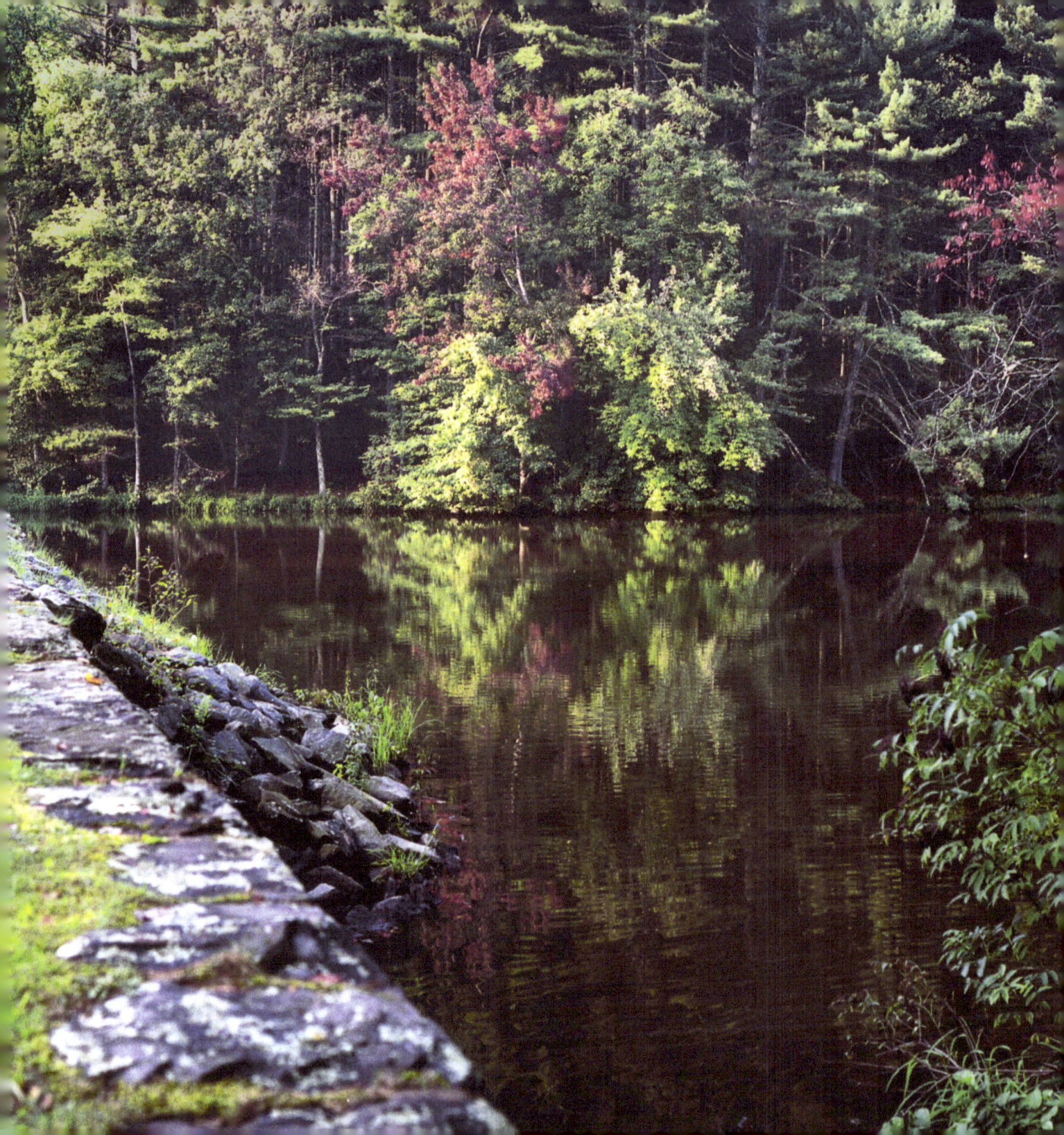

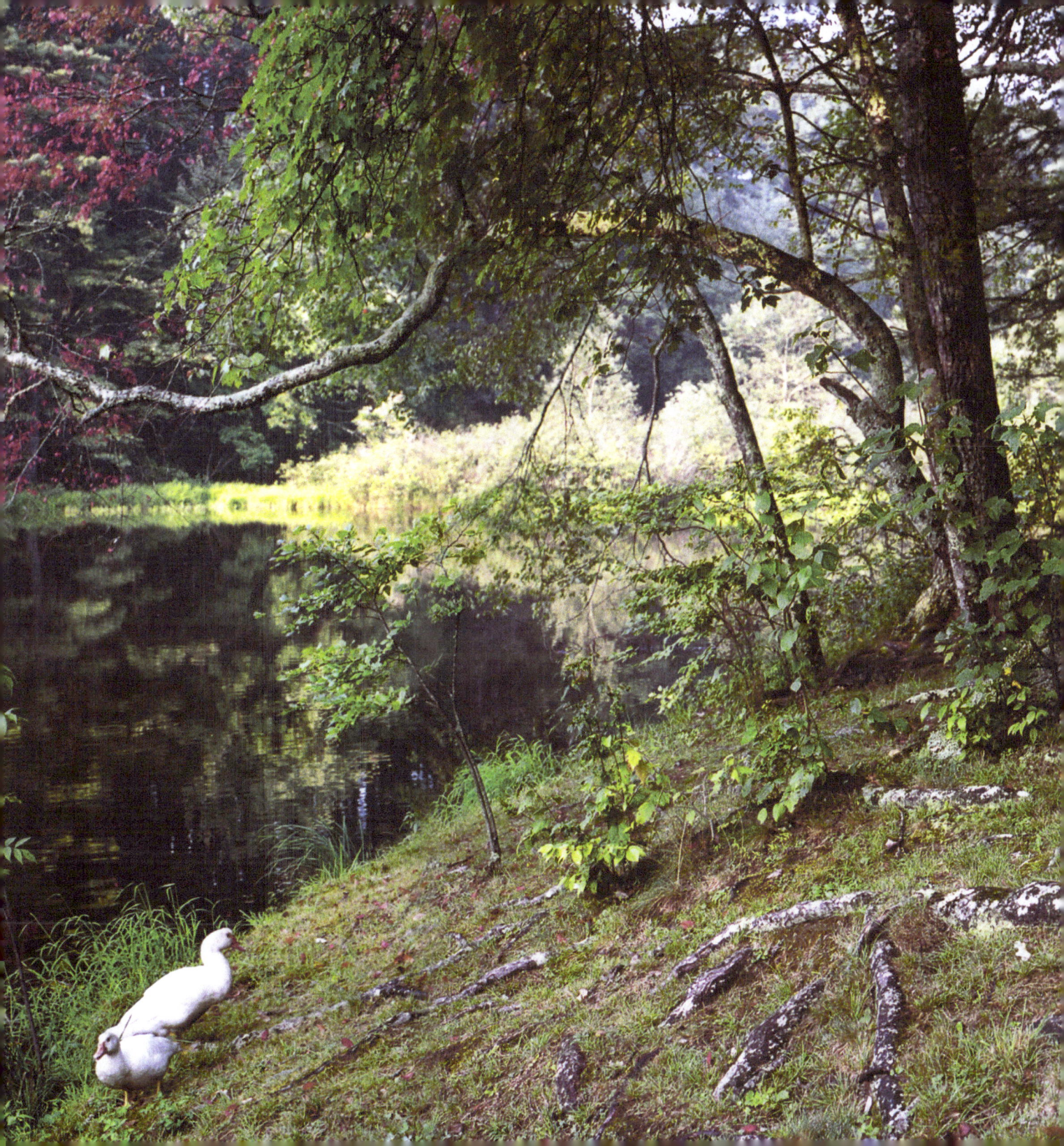

15. **The Shire.**
Blueberry bushes at the old Swansie Shepherd farm
(now Old Orchard Creek Farms) in Ashe County.

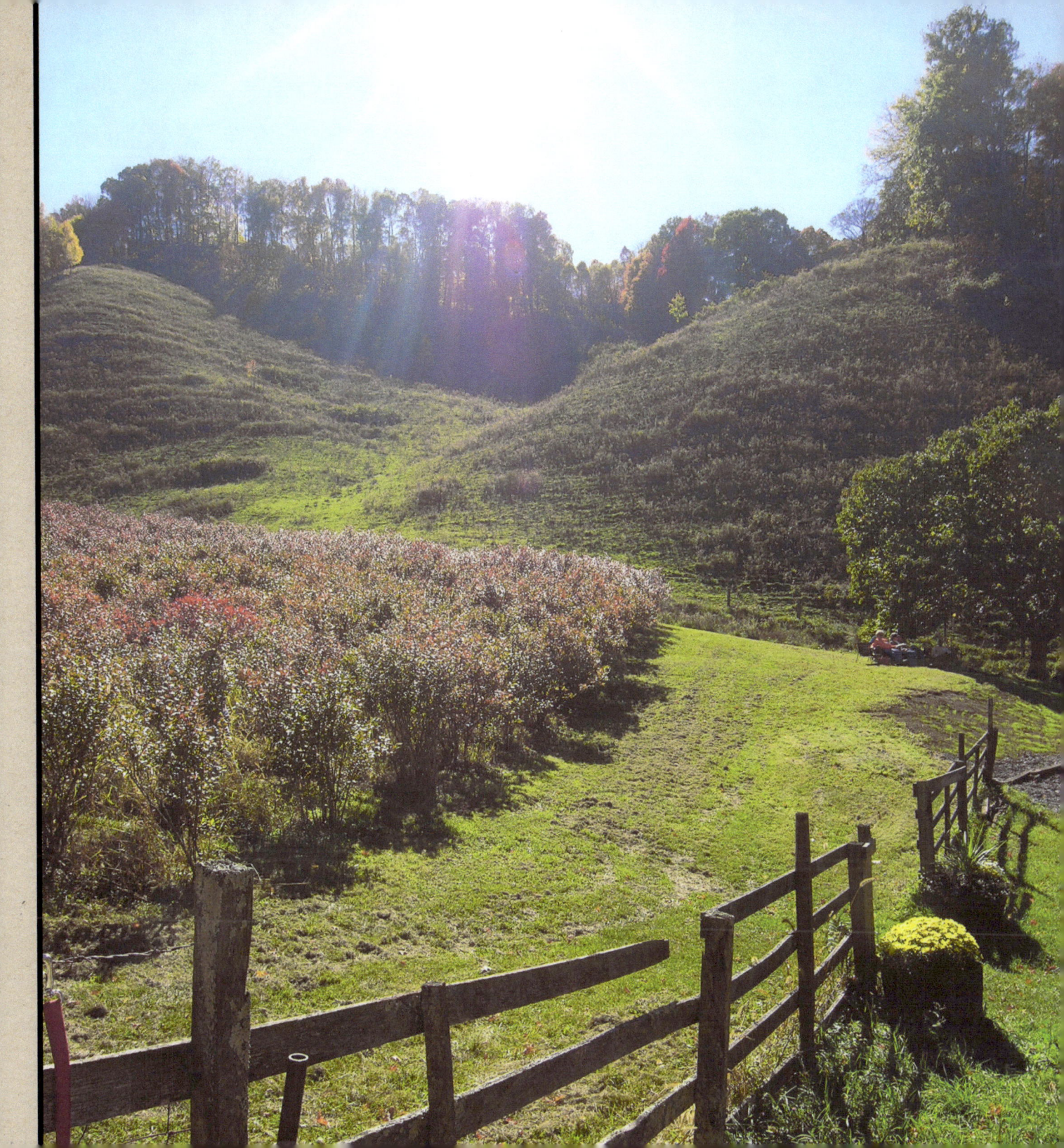

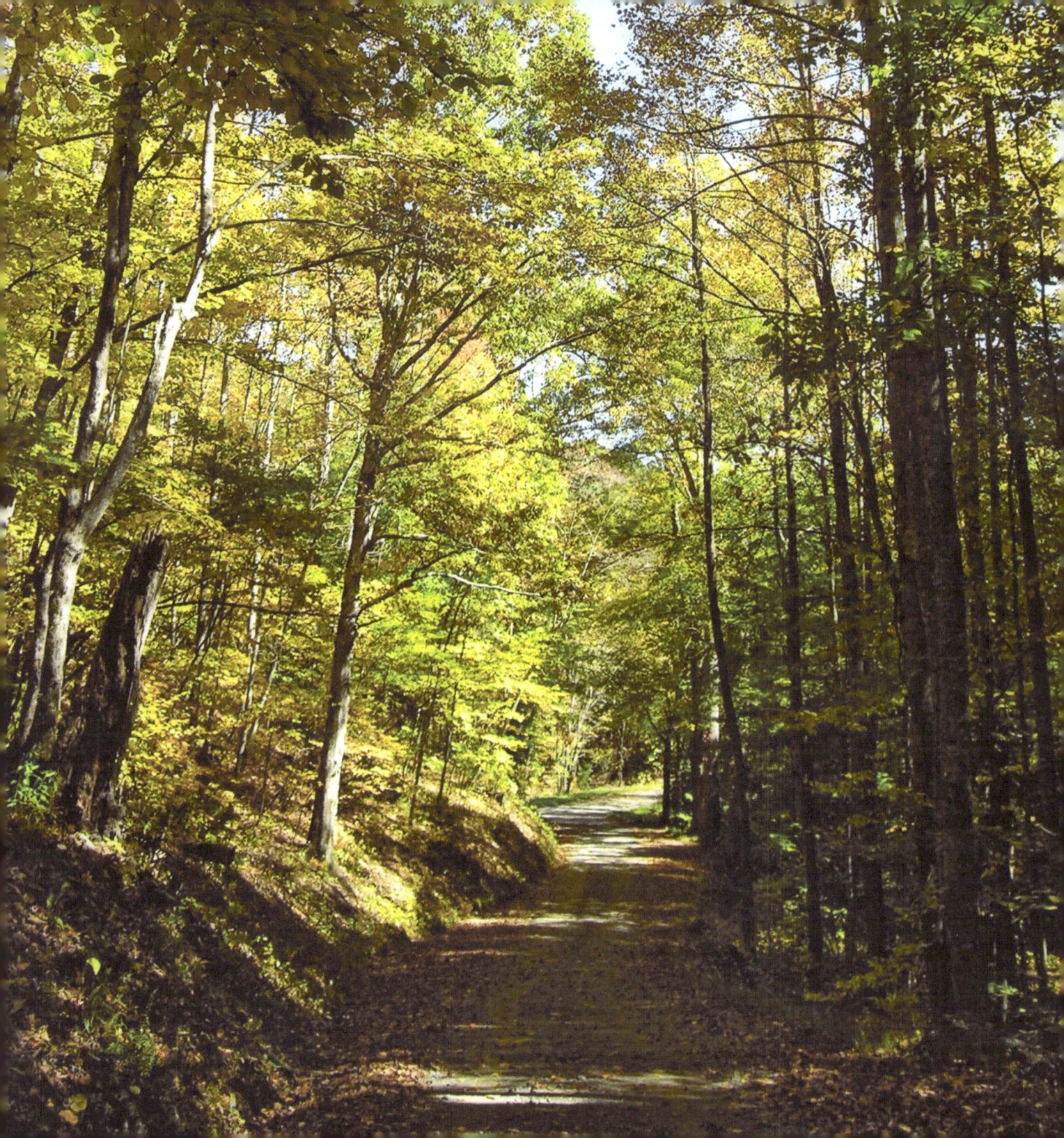

16. **Turning Trees.**
    Nice afternoon on Cheek Mountain Road with an
    almost indoor feeling created by a leafy canopy.

17. & 18. **Untitled Trees 3 and 4**.
    Fiery fall colors made more vibrant by a cobalt blue
    sky. No wind- standing still and waiting for their
    close up. *(Following pages)*

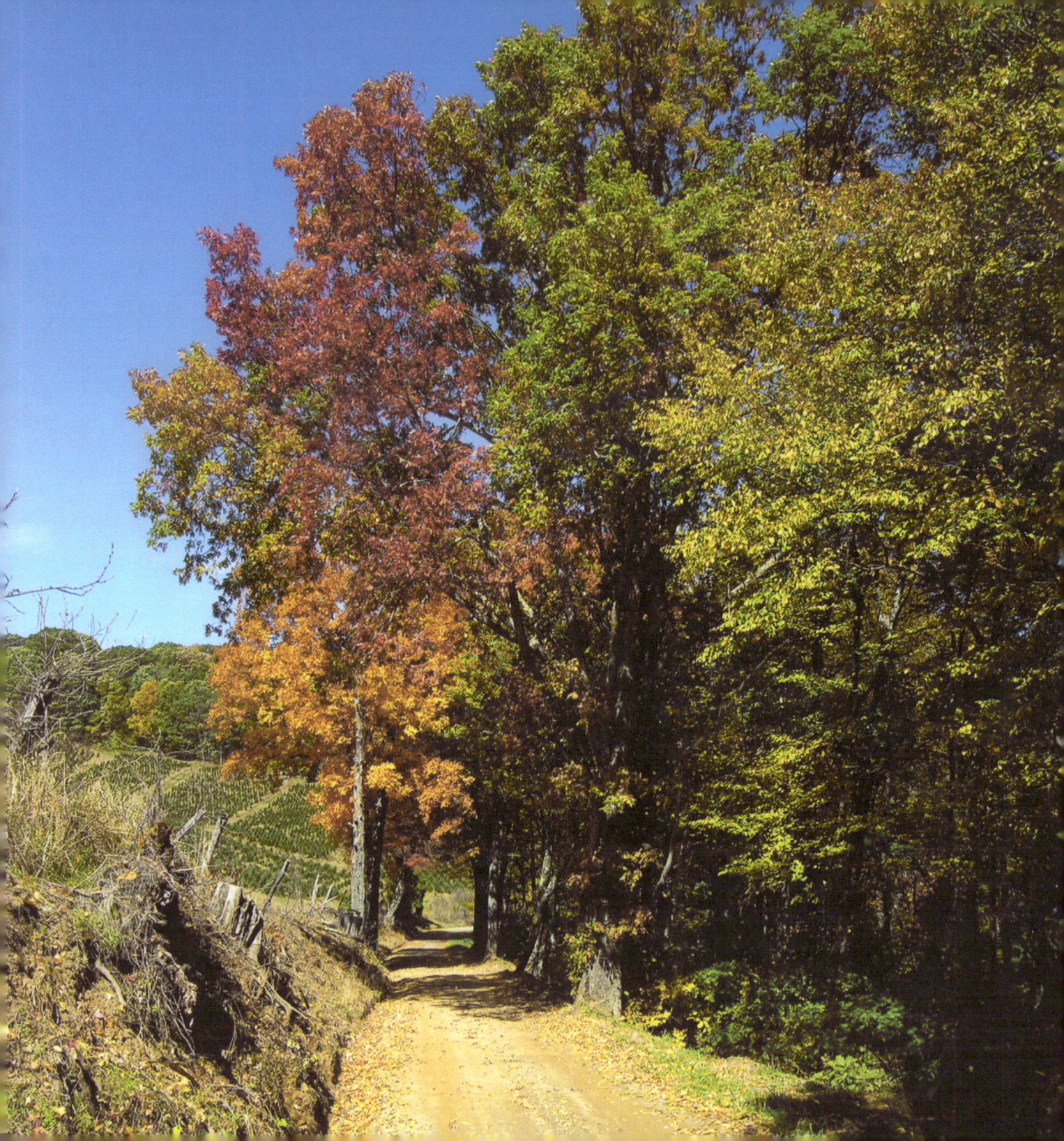

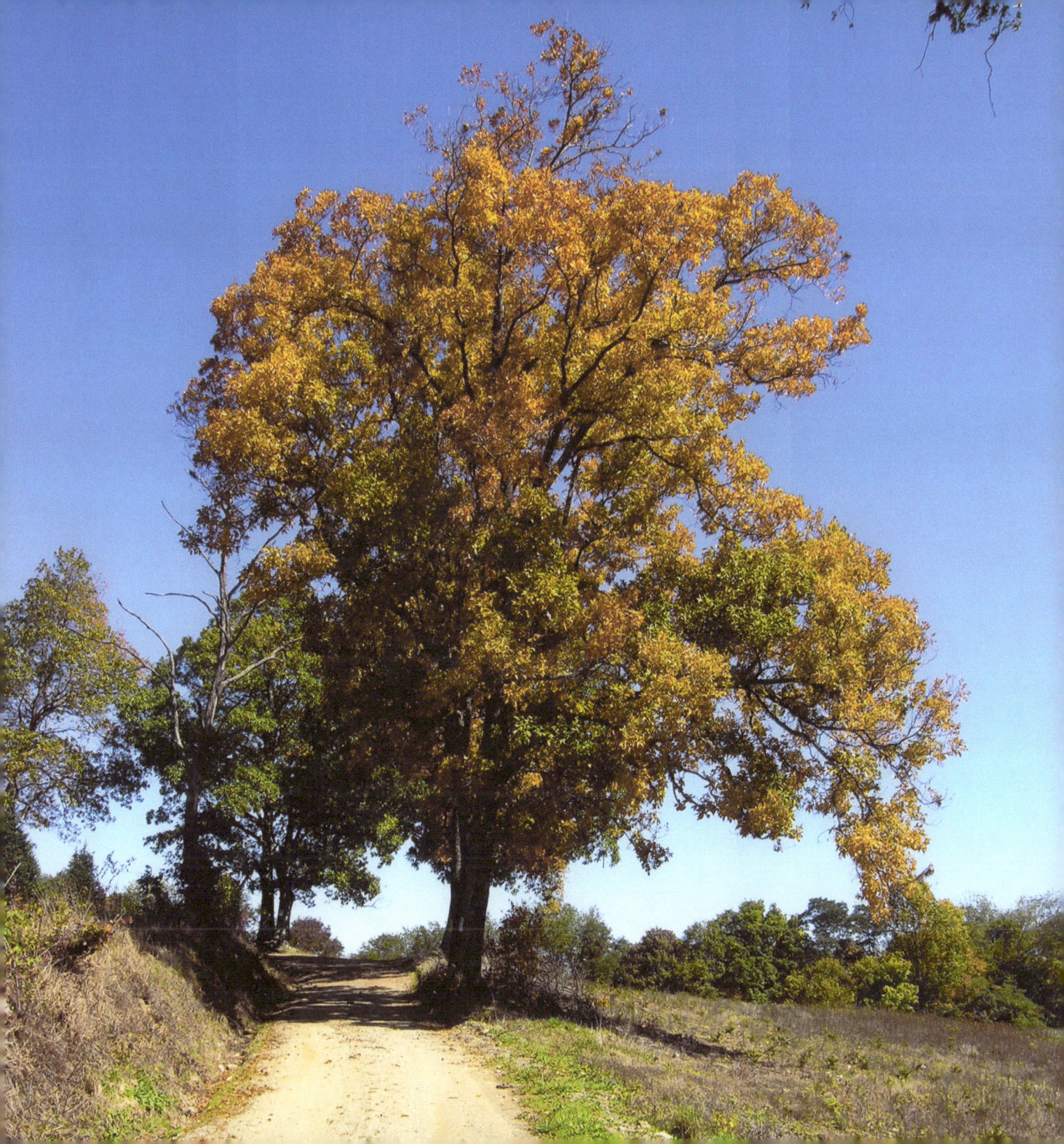

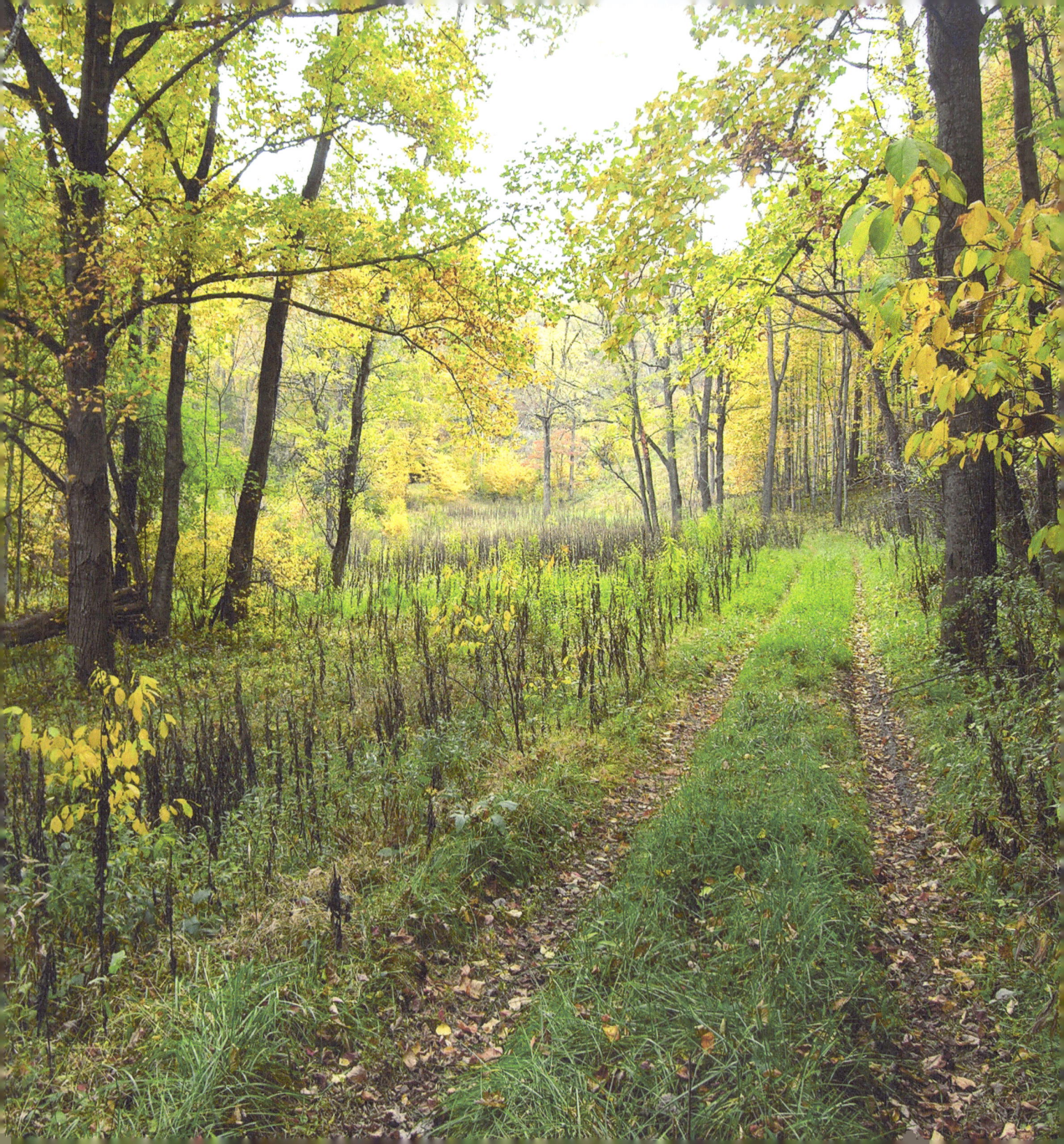

19. **Trespassing**.
    A friend took us to this awesome place in a hidden
    hollow where we weren't necessarily supposed to be.

20. Fall **Road at Air Bellows** just off the Parkway.

21. **Parkway View** at milepost 235, near Air Bellows Gap.
   (Following pages)

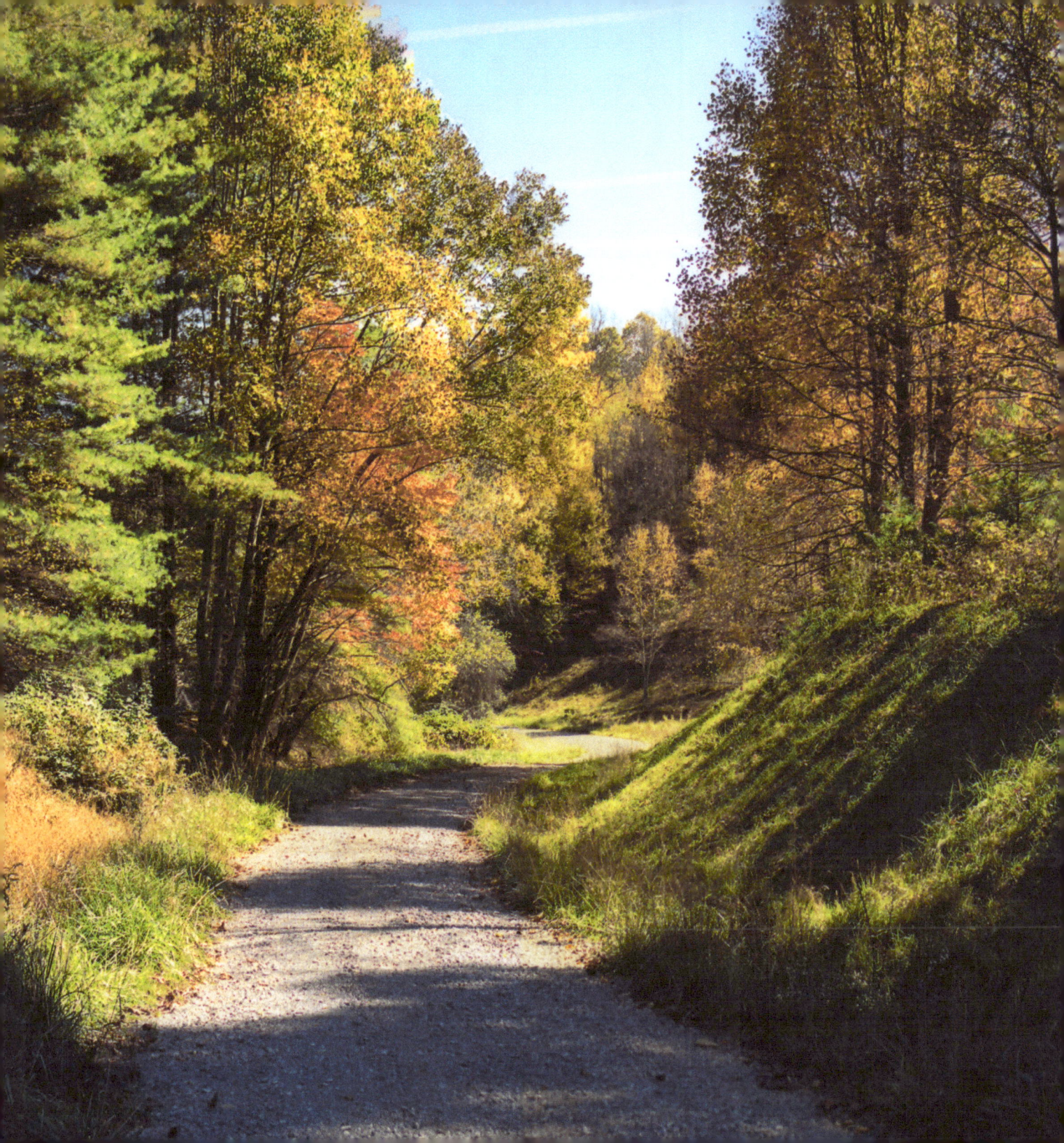

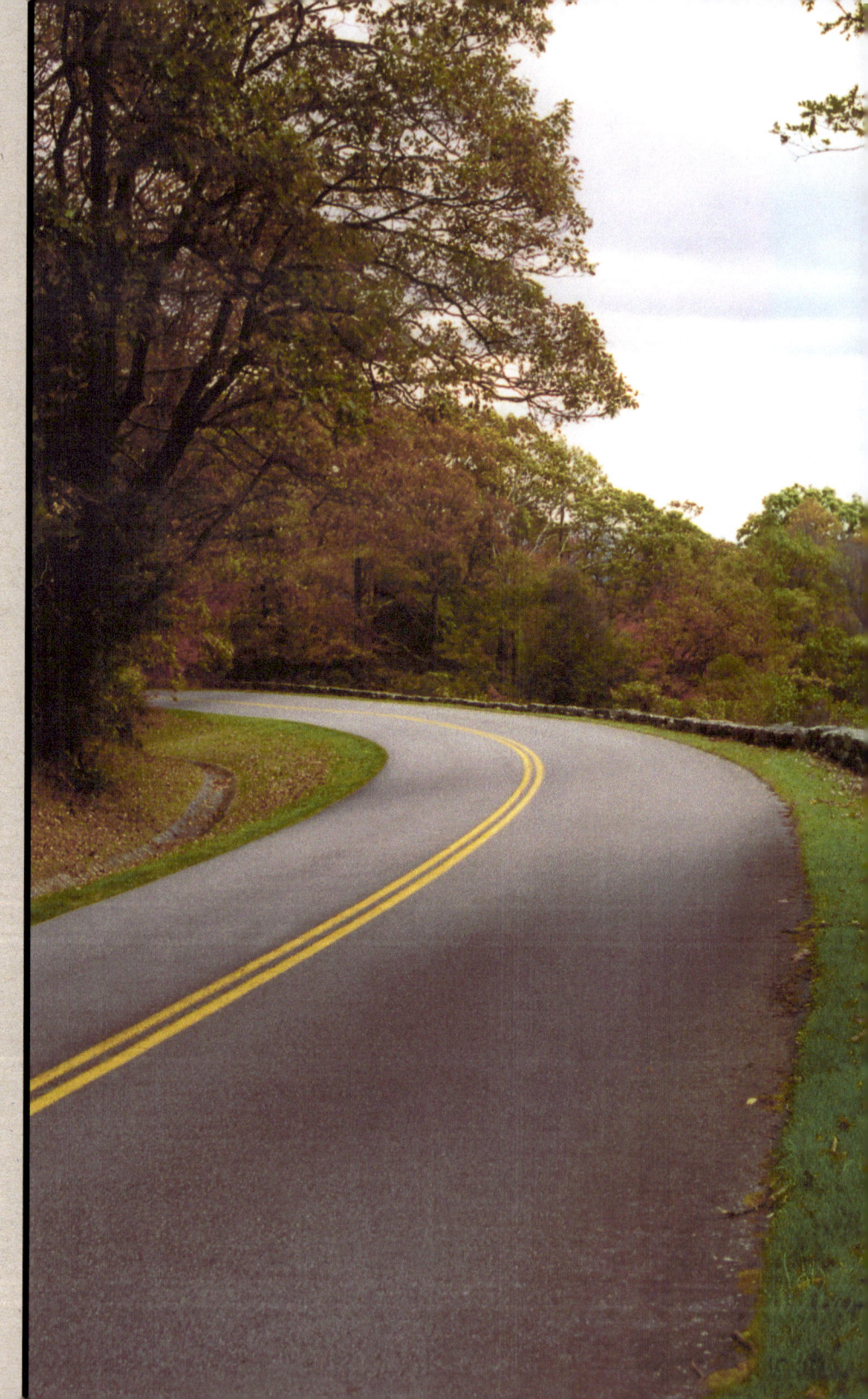

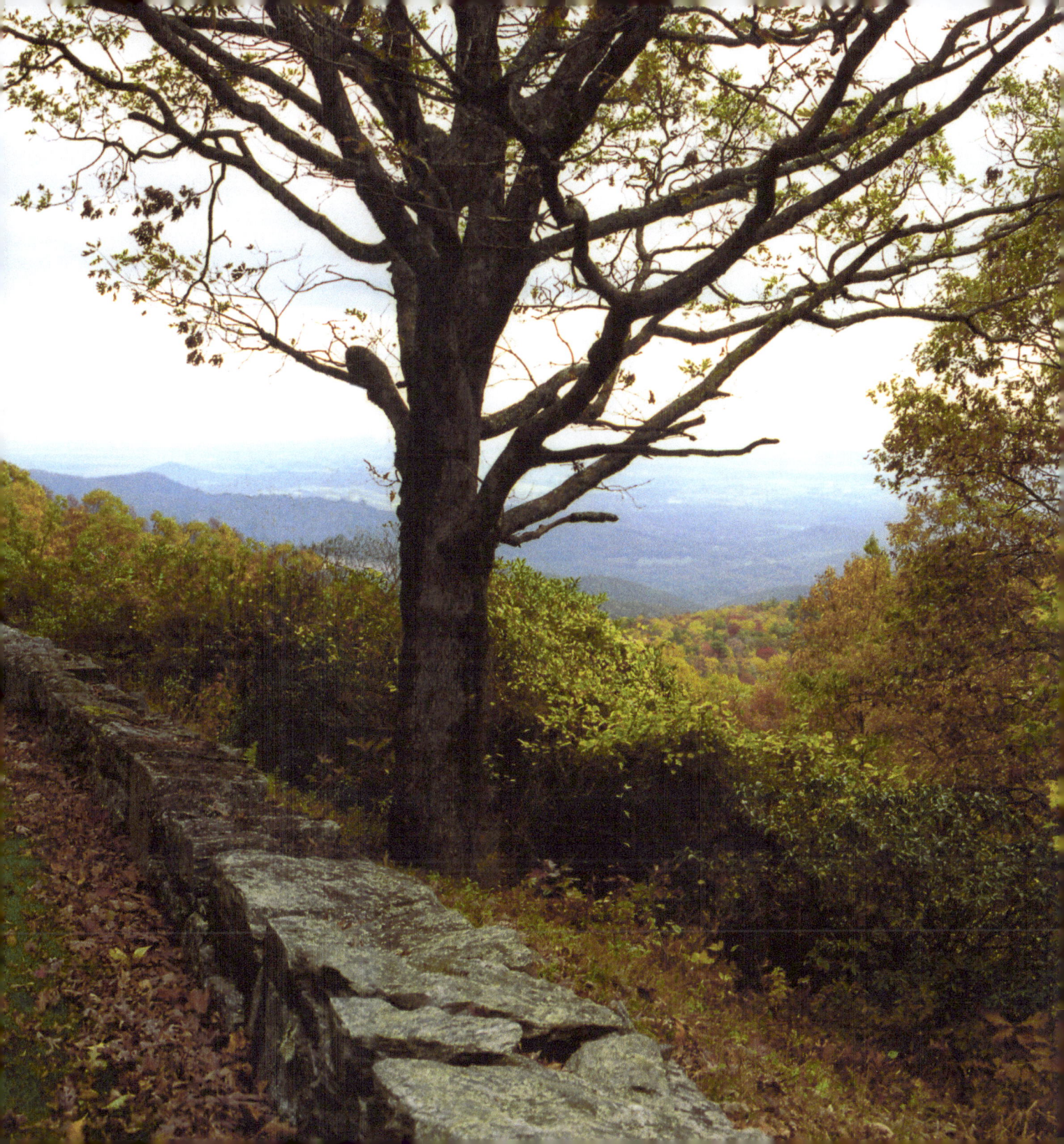

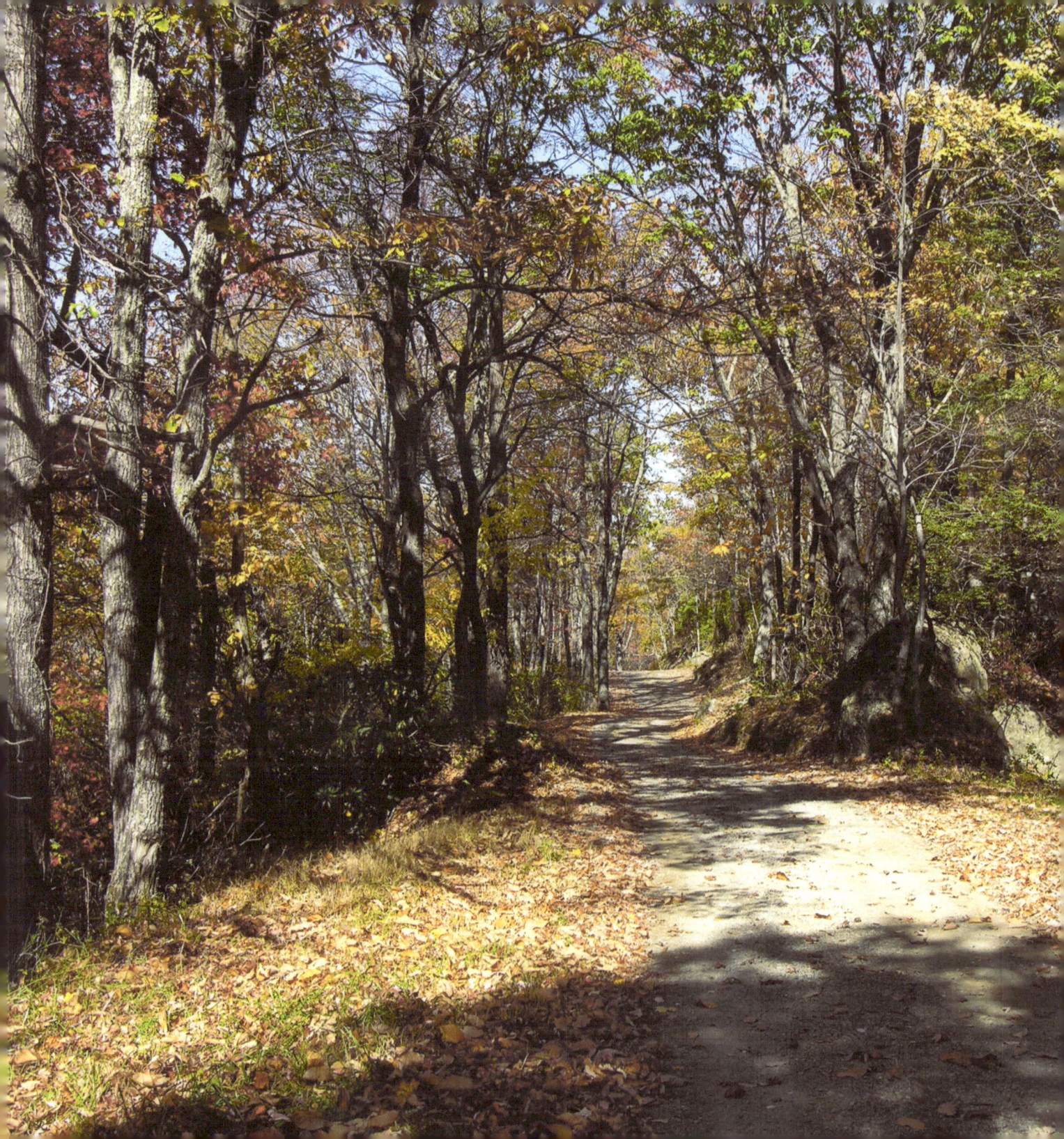

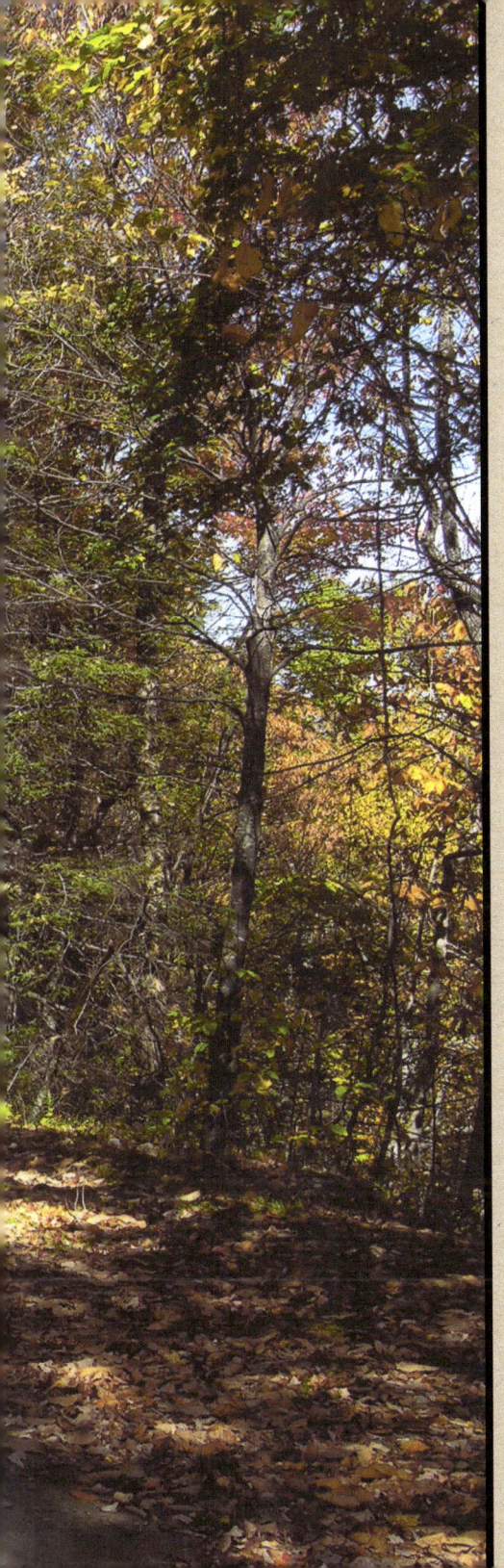

22. **Waterfall Road.**
Late autumn view down the
mountain. The banks fall
off steeply on both sides,
and you can hear the water
trickling somewhere down the
mountain.

23. **Carolyn's Drive**.
I originally saw this in my rear view mirror on the way
to our friend's house.

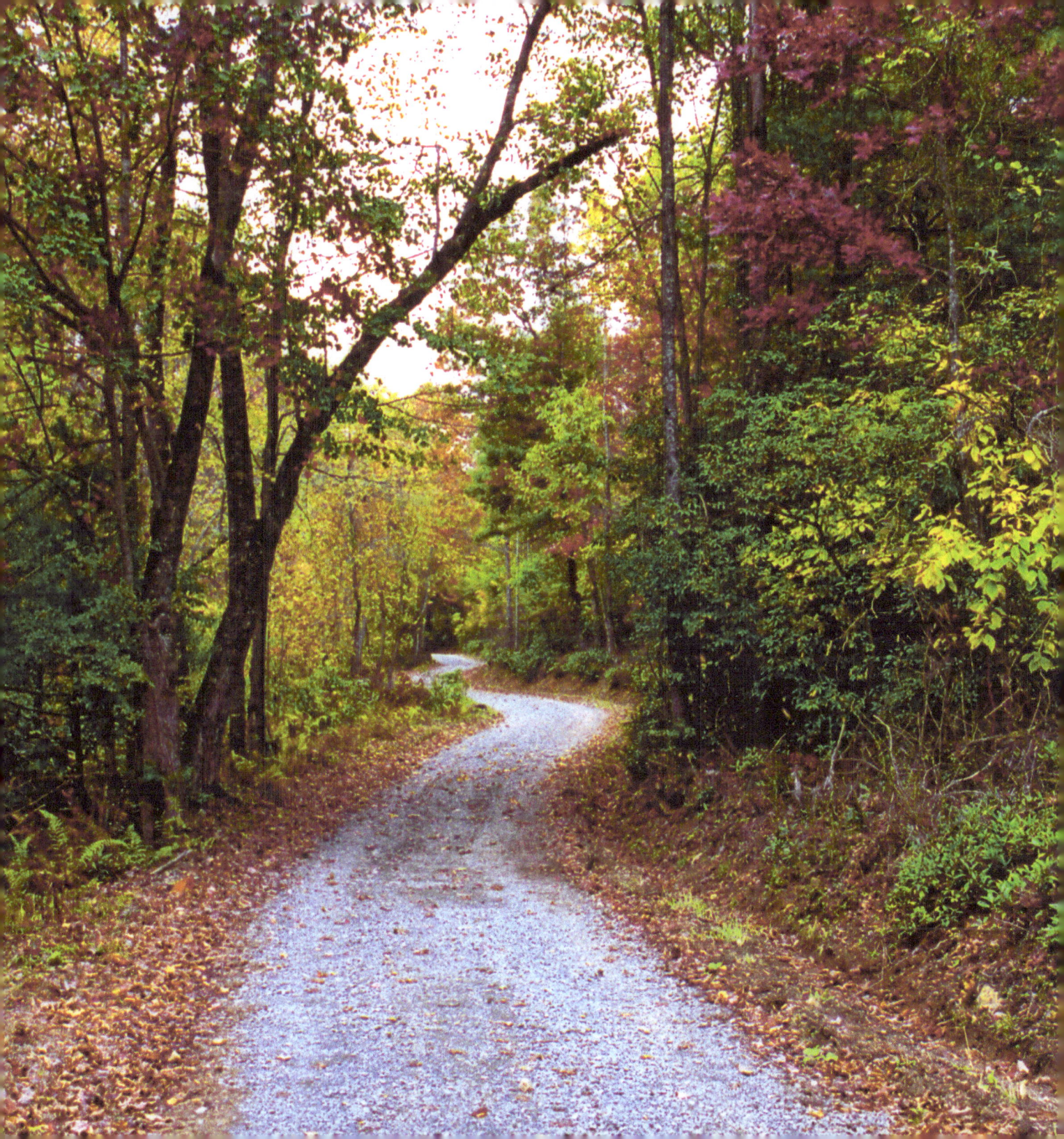

24. **Lonesome Pine** near milepost 233 with fiery sage in a gray drizzle.

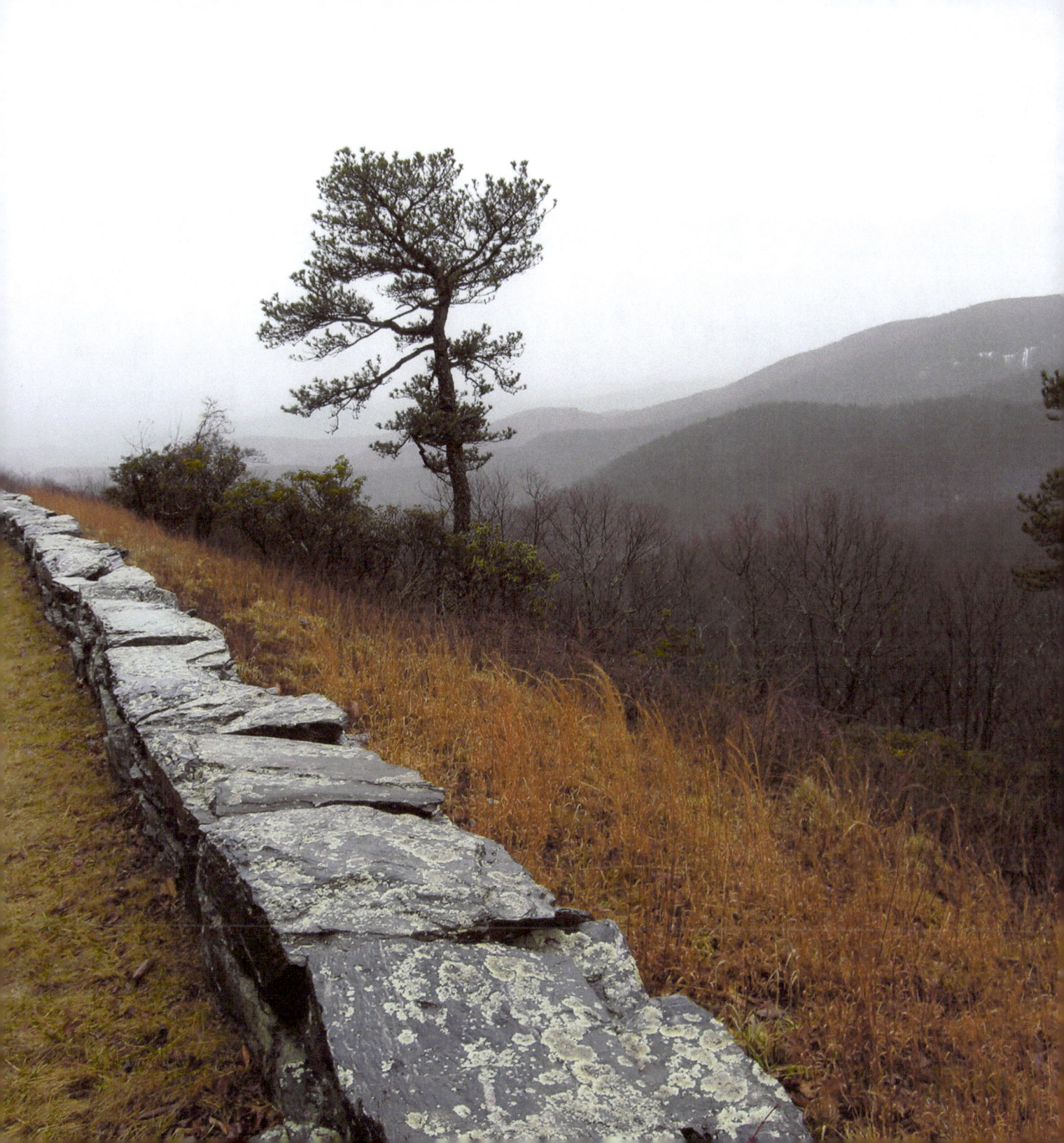

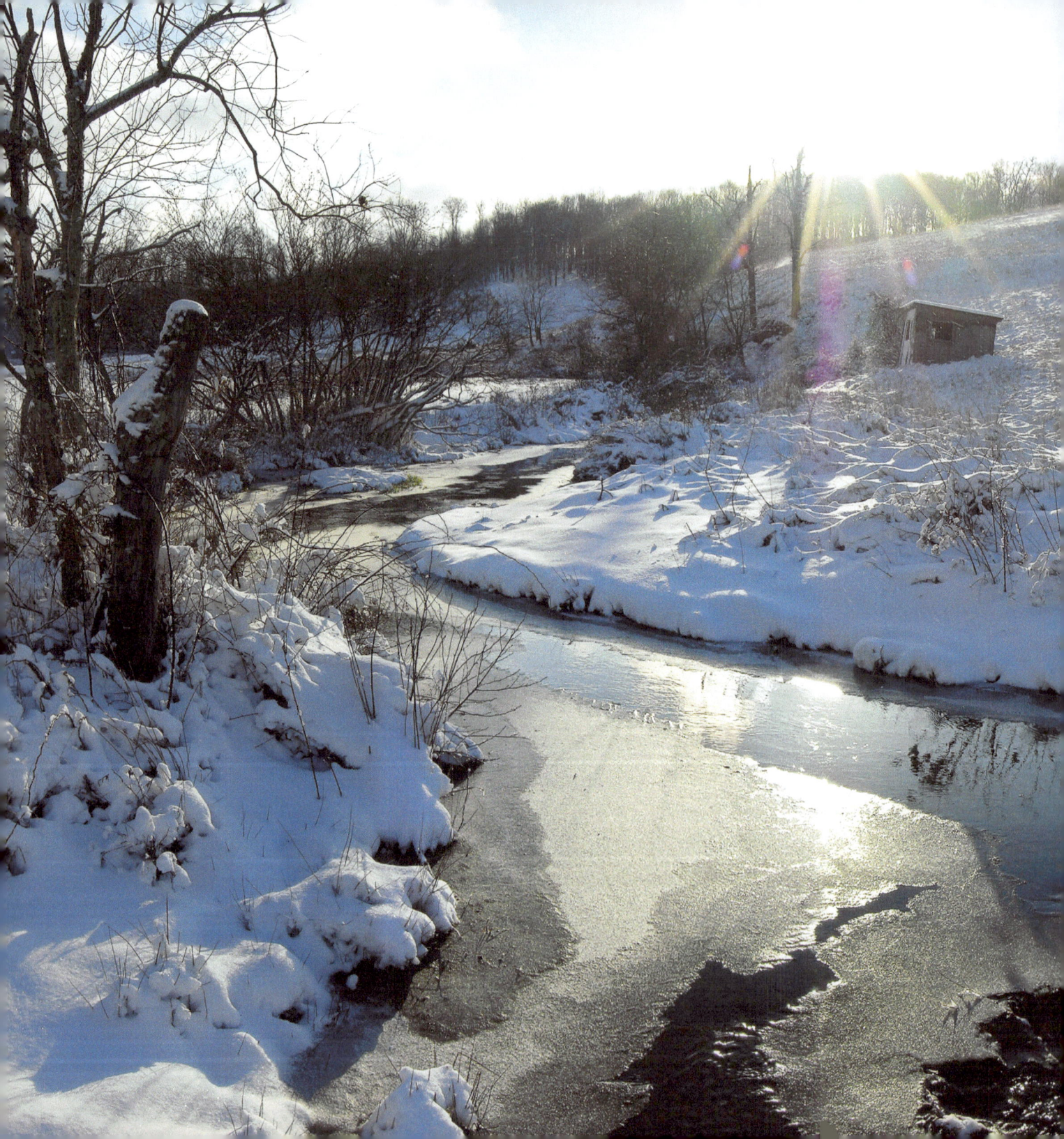

25. **Crystal Creek**.
March snow and ice on Prathers Creek.
Fractured light refracted lightly,
displayed at daytime,
never at nightly.

26. **Walkway On Water**.
Tiny footprints down the bank
and onto the ice in late afternoon
at Hare Mill Pond.

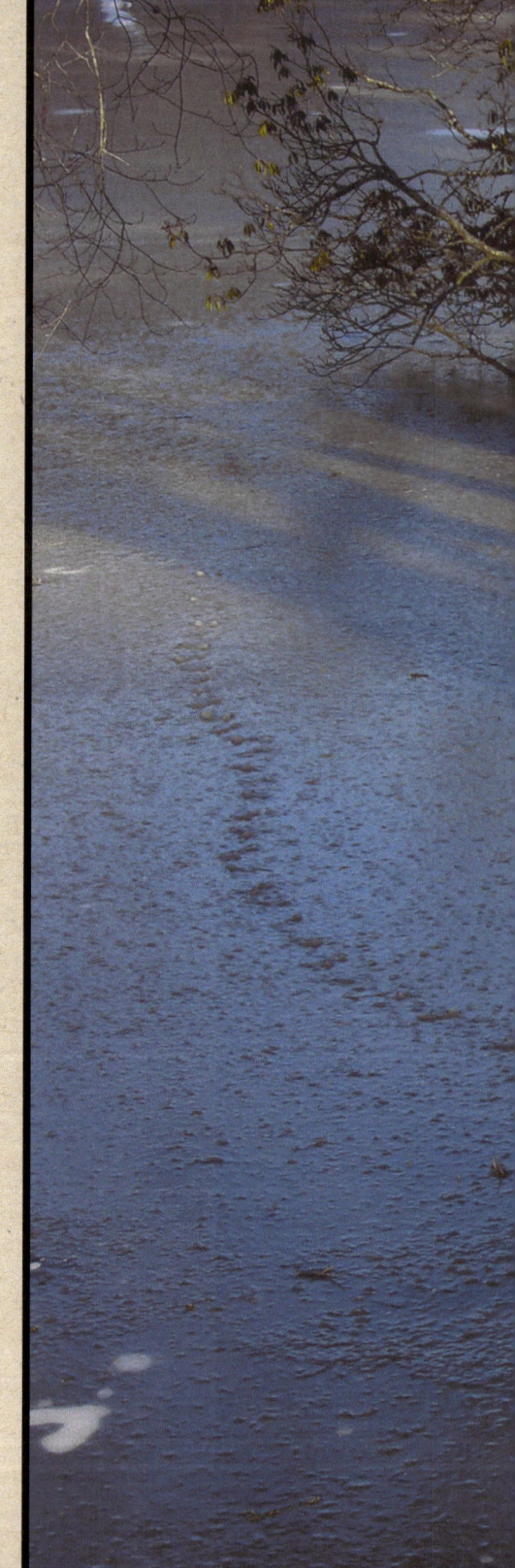

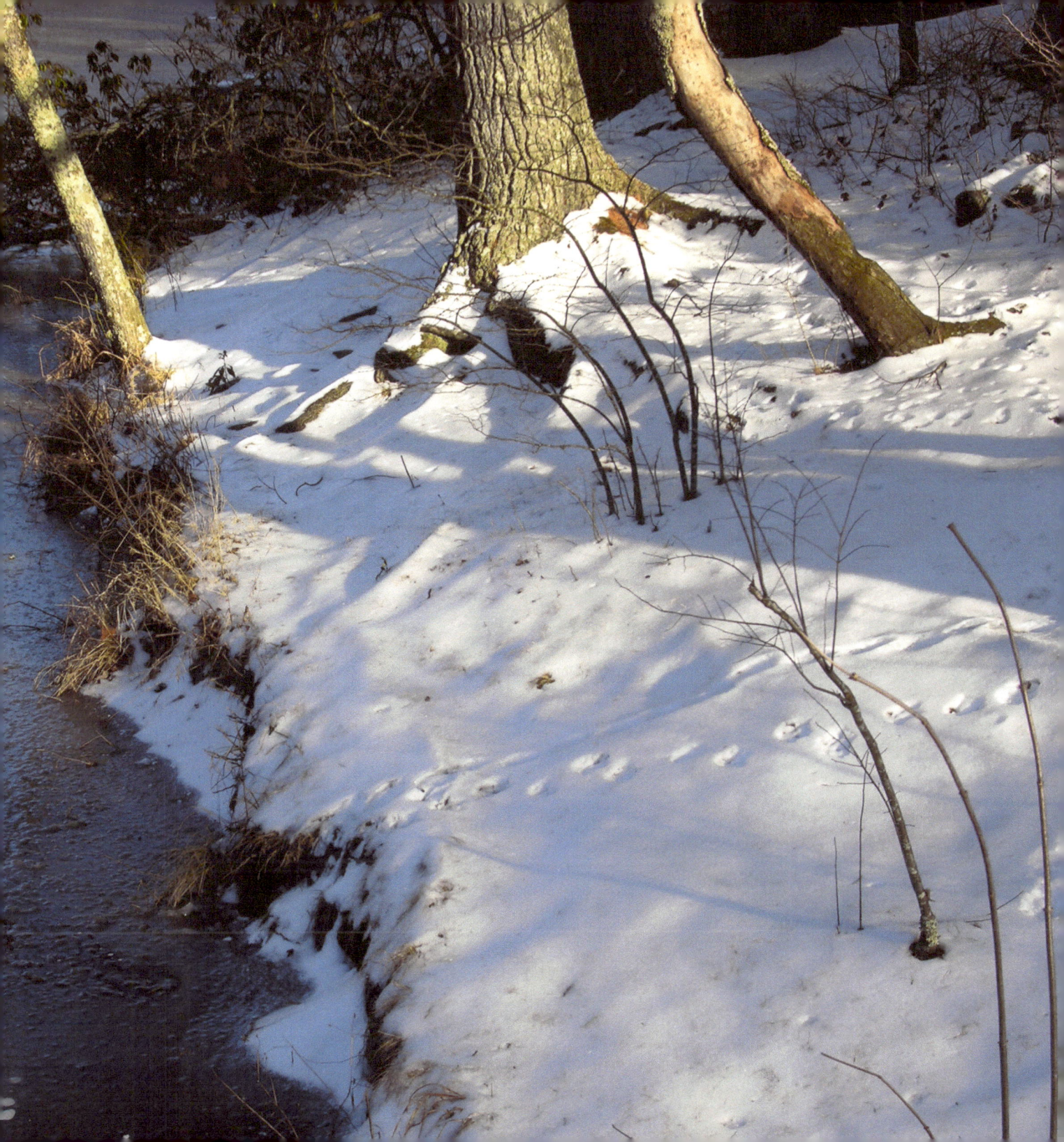

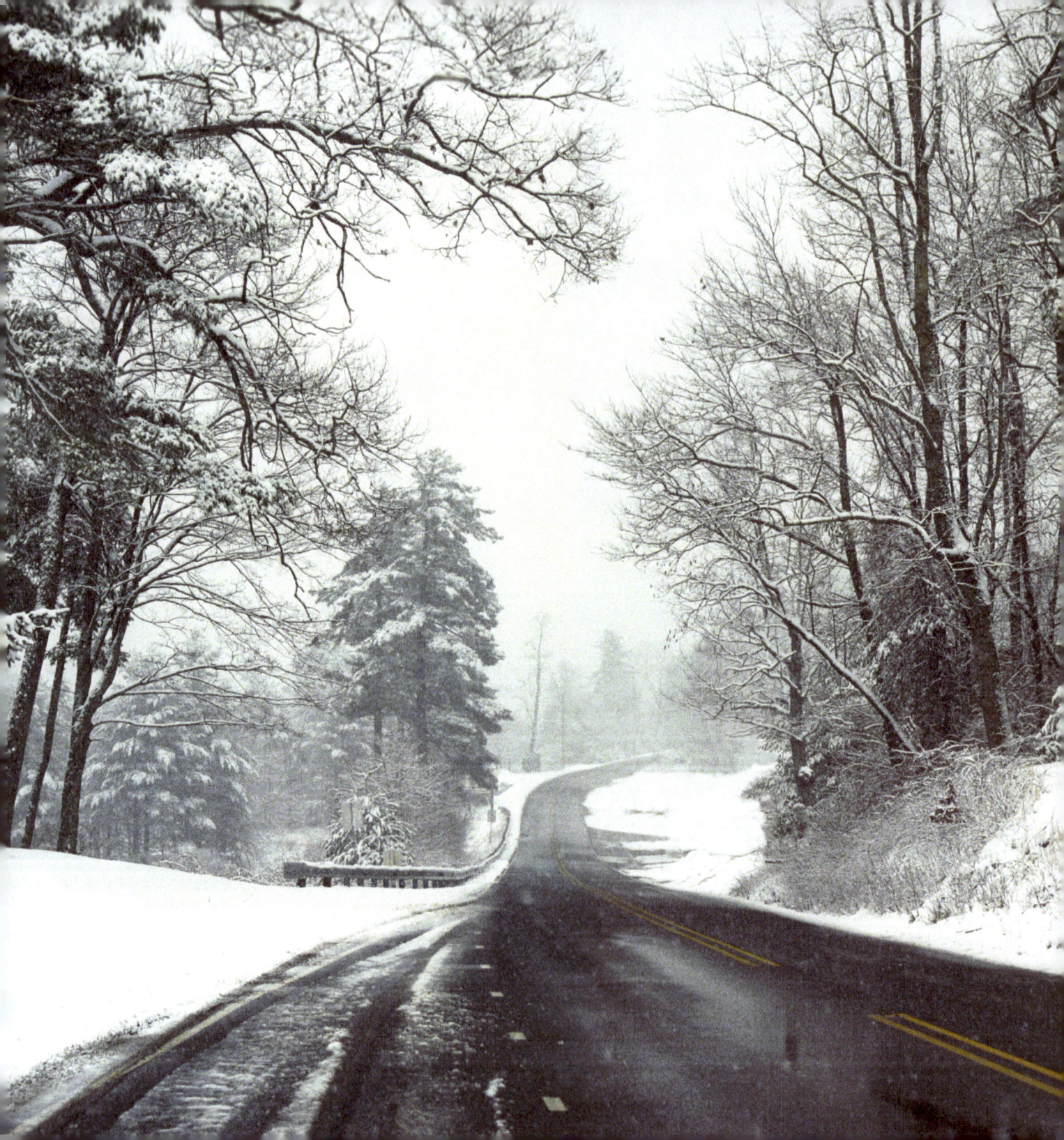

27. **Afternoon Squall** at Roaring Gap. Wet snow on
every branch.

28. The Road Home.

A sunny, snowy, perfect mountain day at New Hope.

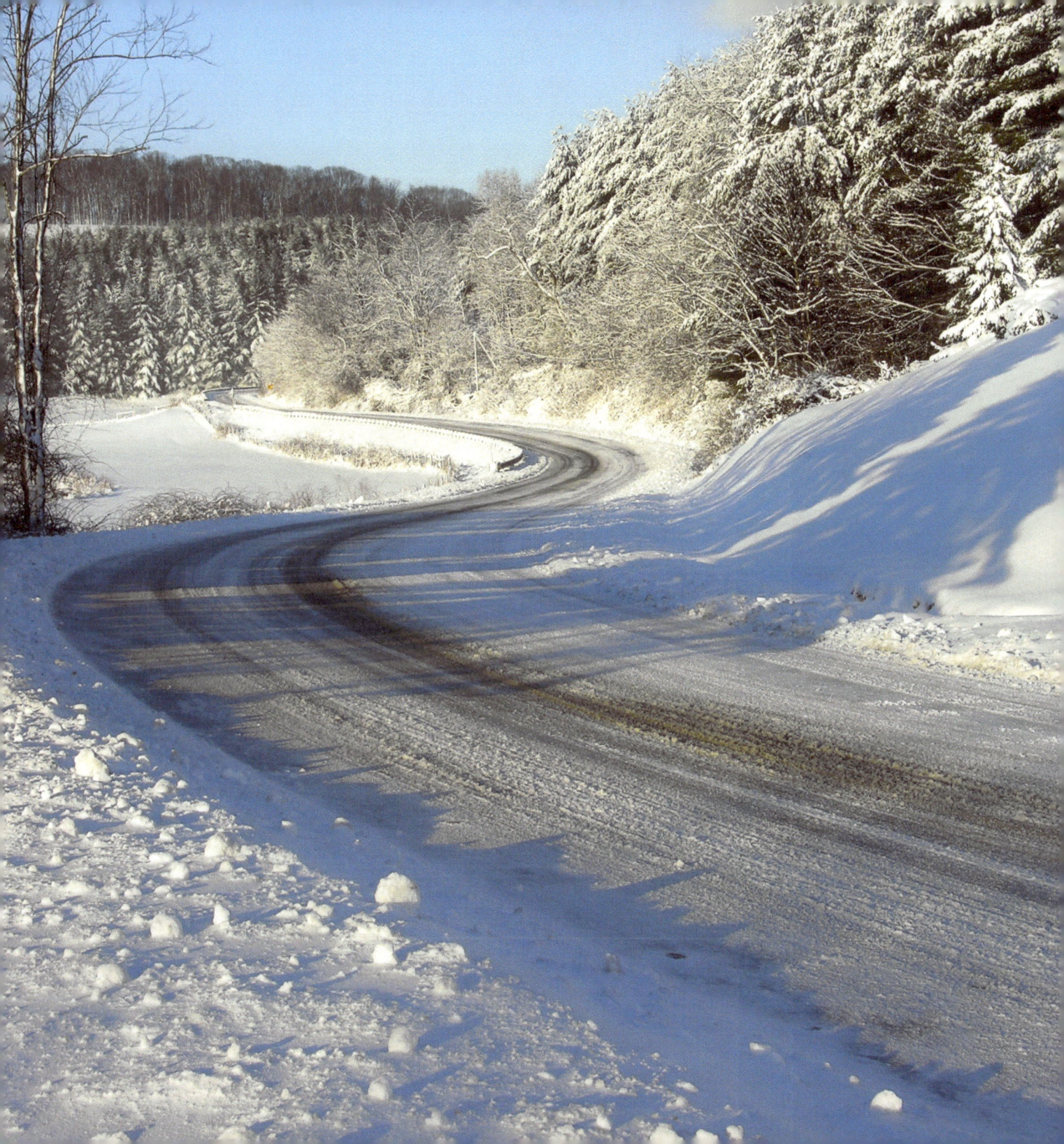

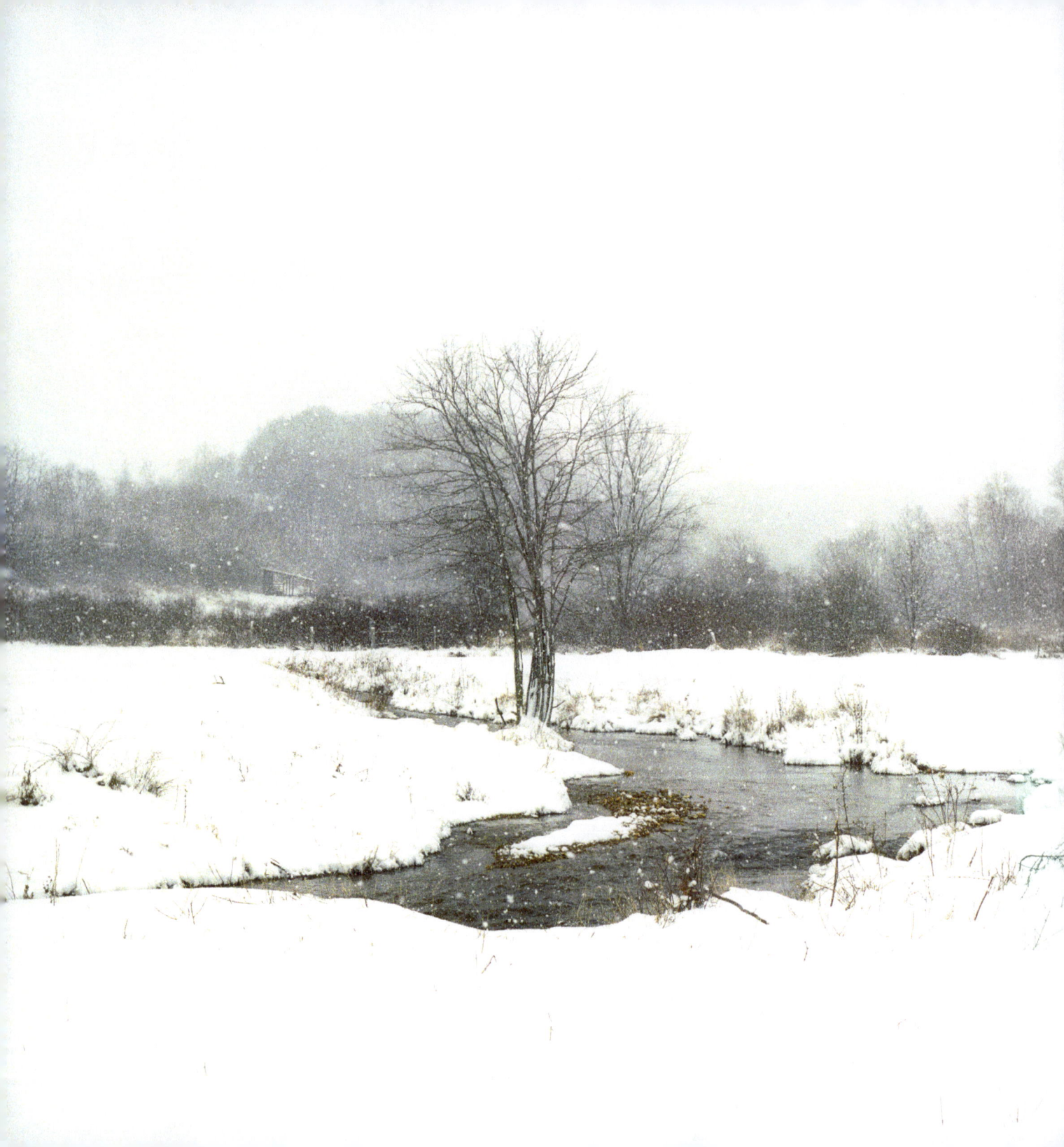

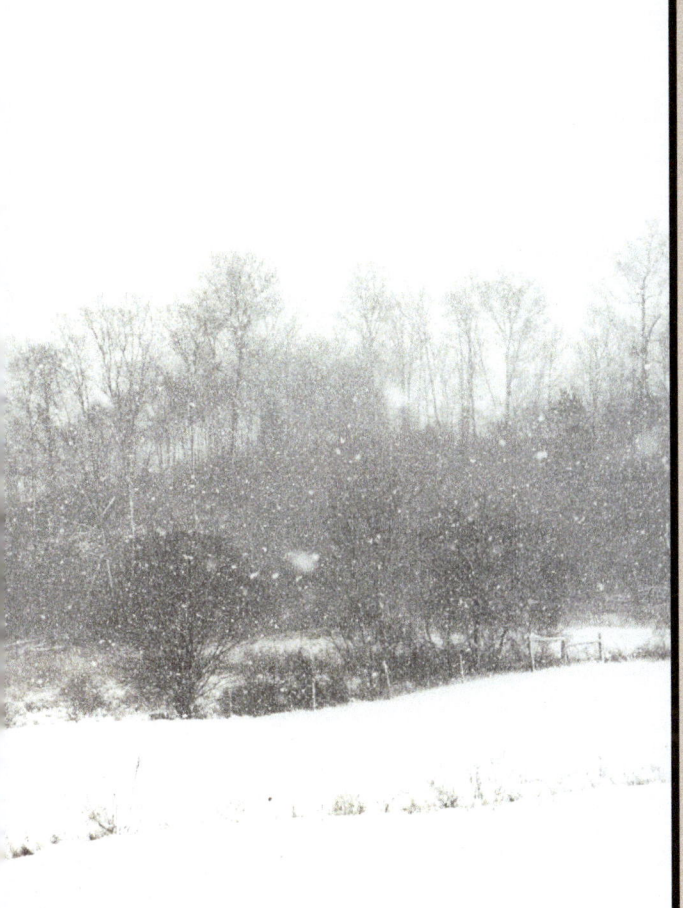

29. **The Treasure Tree**. Winter scene on Prathers Creek. About as far away from wading weather as you can get.

30. **Mr. Green's Farm**. I like the shadows of the trees across the snow and the fences around the barn lot. *(Following pages)*

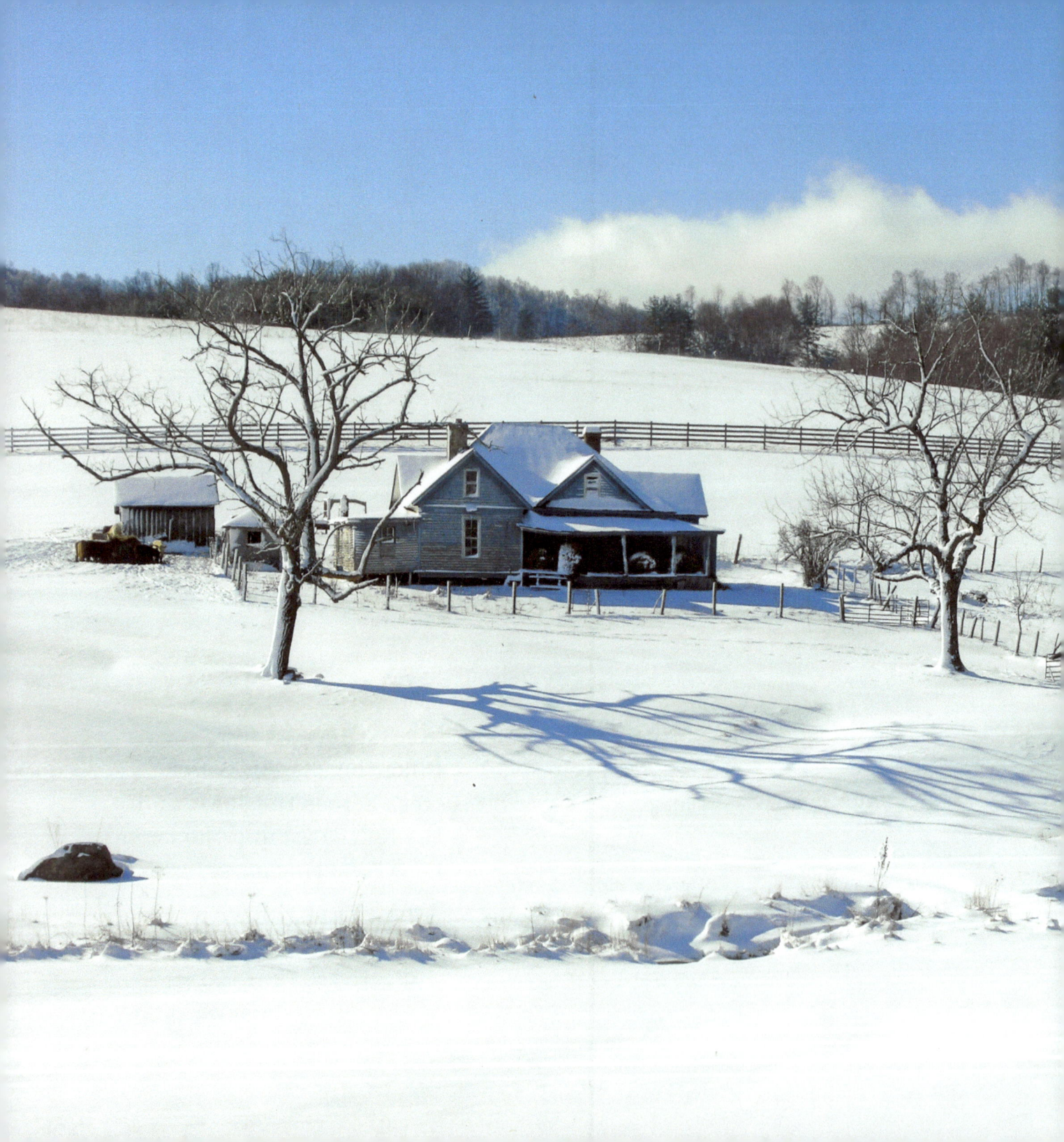

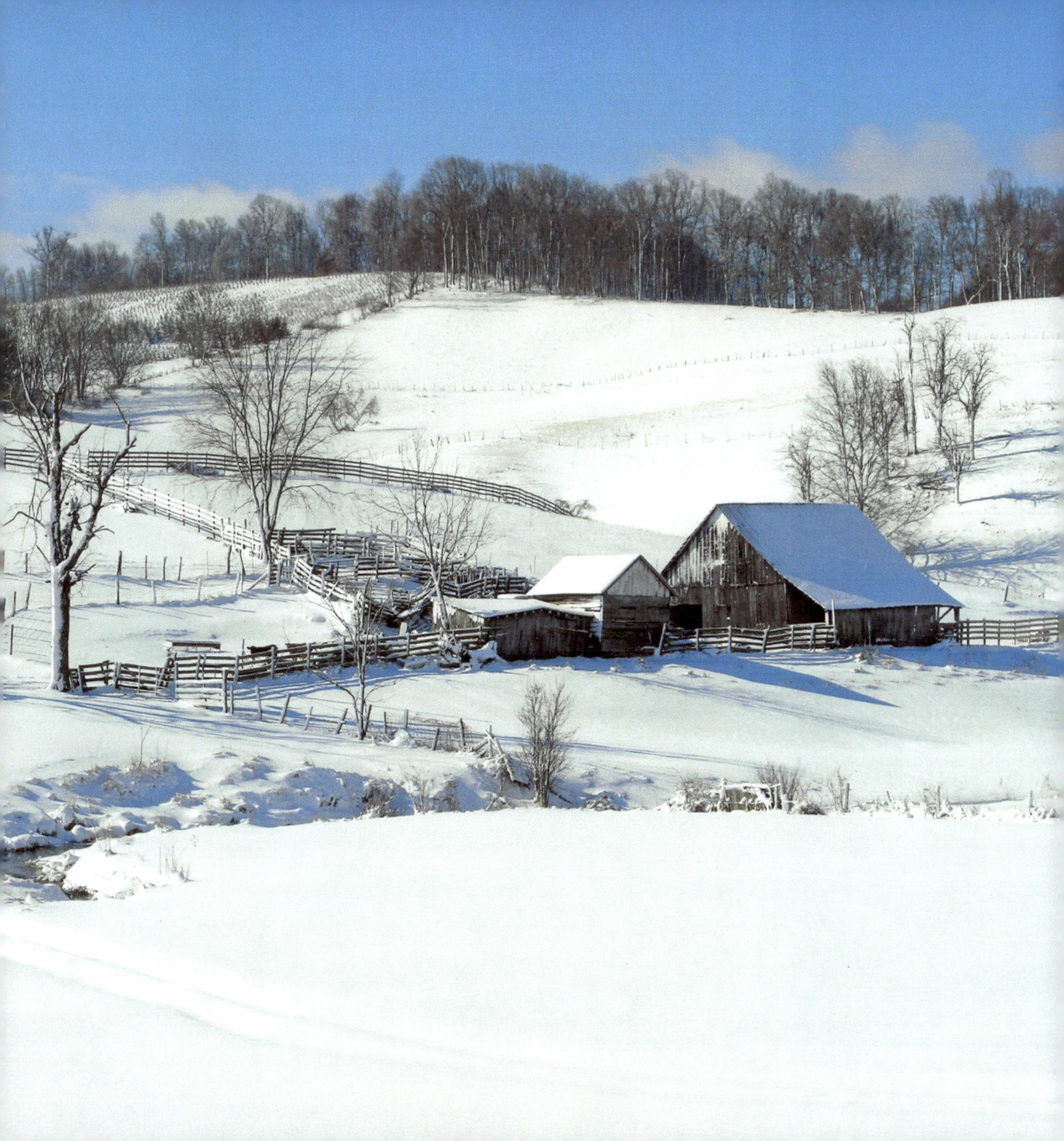

31. **Moon Shadows** at Hare Mill Pond.
We shot this around 8 pm, and it was so cold I couldn't feel the trigger. This is actually Claire's shot. She first saw the moonlight in the snow and called me over. It wouldn't have surprised me to see ice fairies dance across the scene.

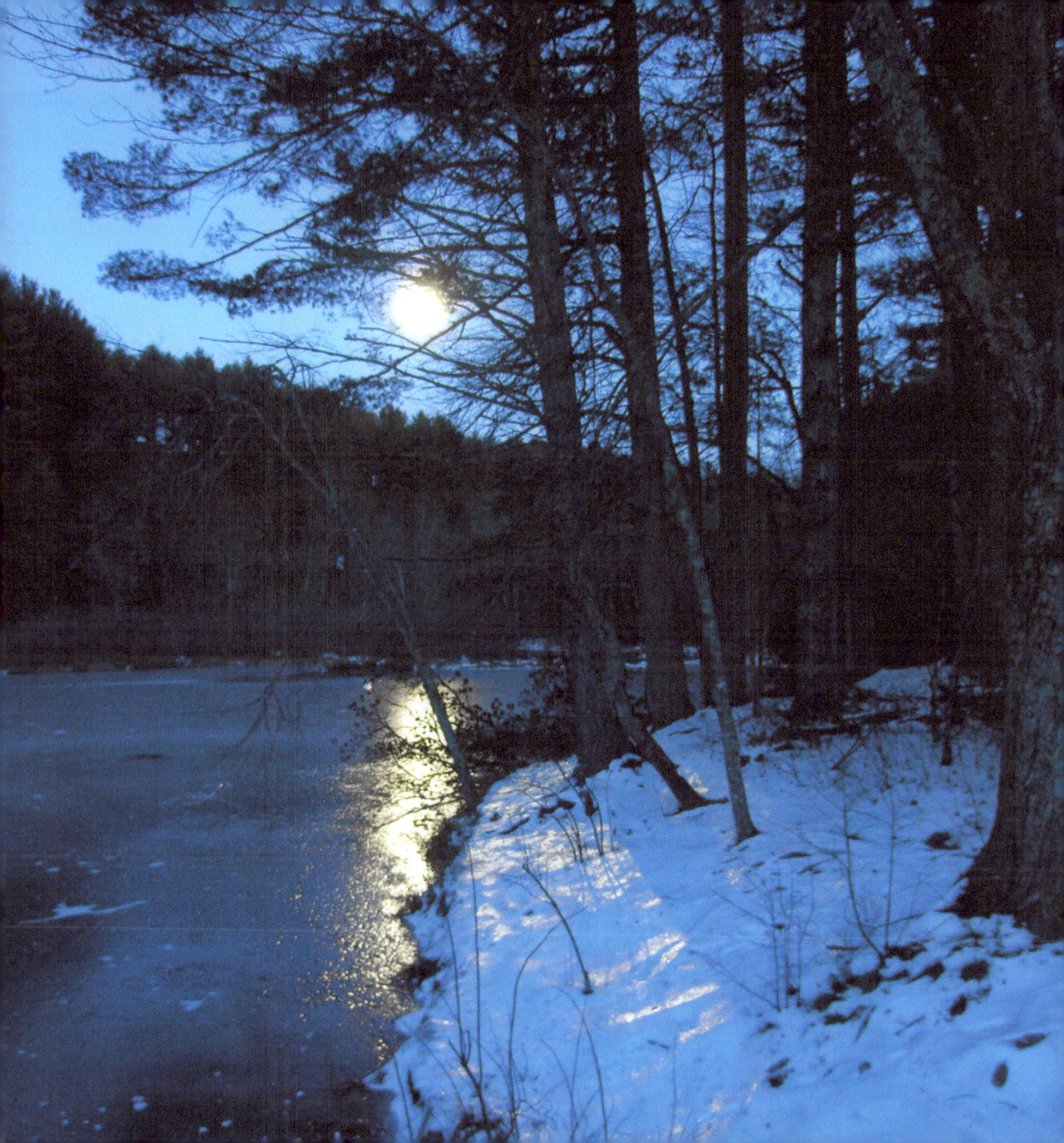

Note

The photography in this collection was all shot in Ashe and Alleghany Counties in upper-northwest North Carolina and includes both film and digital formats. Some images were made from multiple exposures, stitched together manually in Adobe® Photoshop.

For the most part, content hasn't been edited, except for the removal of two houses from the photo, Shiloh Rainbow on page 8. The white houses were comparatively over exposed and were distracting. A dry brush filter was applied to the Beaver Dam photo on page 24.

Some images are part of larger pans and have been cropped to fit this book's format. All photography, editing, page layout and design by Imaging Specialists, Inc. in Sparta, North Carolina.

For more information, please visit:
starroutebooks.com or imagingspecialists.net

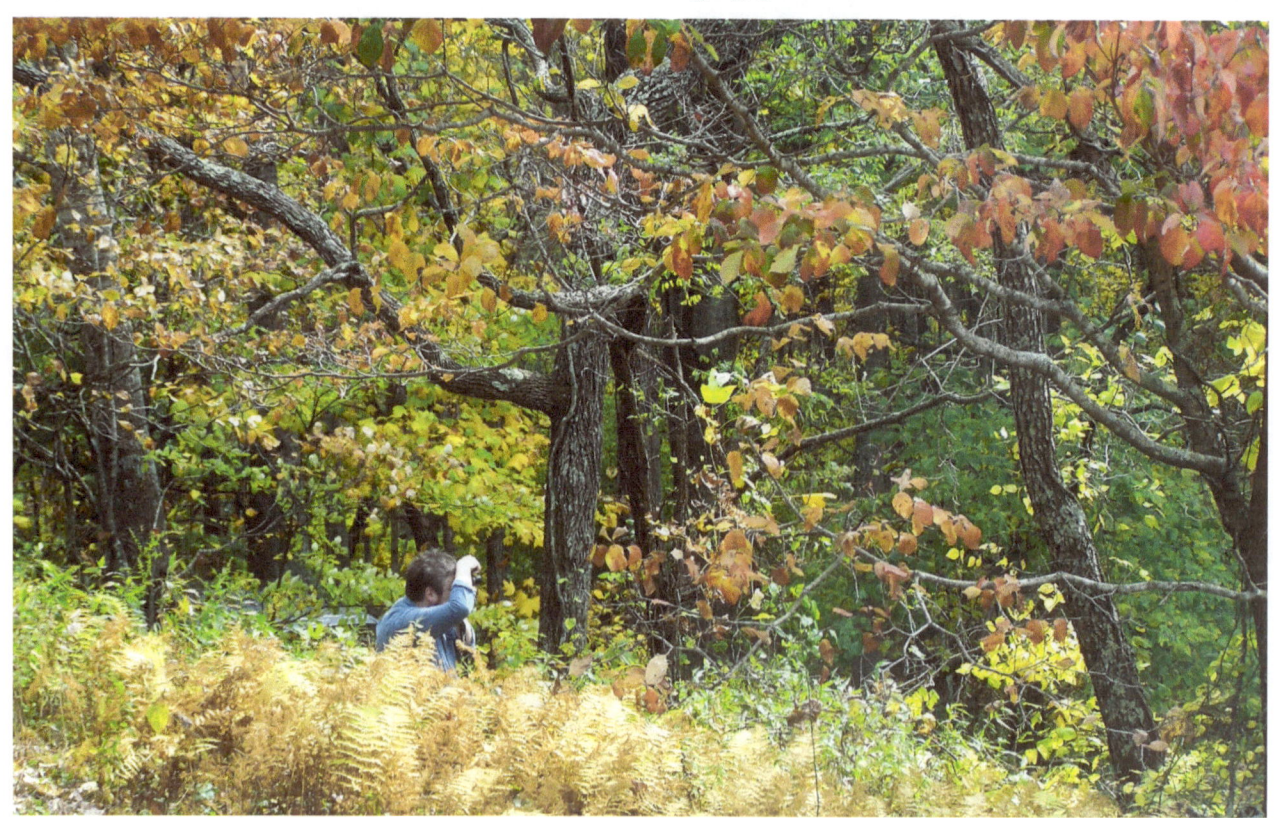

Photo by Claire Halsey

www.ingramcontent.com/pod-product-compliance
Lightning Source LLC
Chambersburg PA
CBHW050747180526
45159CB00003B/1377